EARS TO HEAR EYES TO SEE

Witnessing Through Media

DON BOULDIN

BROADMAN PRESS
Nashville, Tennessee

Dewey Decimal Classification: 248.5
Subject Headings: WITNESSING // CHURCH MEDIA LIBRARIES
Library of Congress Catalog Card Number: 87-8057
Printed in the United States of America

Library of Congress Cataloging-in-Publication Data

Bouldin, Don, 1938-
    Ears to hear, eyes to see.

    1. Mass media in religion.   I. Title.
BV652.95.B68   1987   253'.7   87-8057
ISBN 0-8054-3002-4 (pbk.)

Preface: Especially for Pastors

Hey Pastor! What would you do if someone made you an offer you couldn't refuse? Well, that's what you are about to get. So read on!

Everywhere I go the word is out. Pastors and church workers of every variety and persuasion are complaining about the enormity of the work and the limitations of the help. To put that another way . . . there is too much to be done and too few who are willing to pitch in and do the job. I believe Jesus warned about that when He looked out on the harvest of lost men and women who were "harassed and helpless, like sheep without a shepherd." Then He said to his disciples:

"The harvest is plentiful but the workers are few. Ask the Lord of the harvest, therefore, to send out workers into his harvest field" (Matt. 9:37-38).

People everywhere are in great need. Christians, for the most part, see the need. Sermons call attention to it and urge people to get involved. We hear appeals of thunder from our pulpits to practice "servant" life-styles. But the response to that kind of injunction is limited. Agreed?

Well, I'm here to make you an offer you can't refuse! You may not know it but there are some people in your congregation who have been volunteering for years, but someone keeps telling them to go to the end of the line. Pastor, these are people who are equipped. They have the commitment. Their resources are vast. For years they have been training to do just the job you need done. They are organized and ready to go. When you give the word, they are ready to assist you in getting the job done.

A number of years ago I was just like many of you. Overworked, burdened, harassed, short-handed, I often had the feeling that no one really understood the plight of the pastor. Maybe no one really cared! Somehow the people I pastored seemed to assume it was my task to evangelize the lost, disciple those who were won, and prod, push, and shove the average church member into doing "his ministry." I really had the feeling that the perception of the majority of my flock was that I was to be a one-man show. To say I was frustrated is an understatement!

God's timing is perfect! That summer a whole series of events radically altered my perspective. Keith Mee is a manager in the Church Media Library Department of the Baptist Sunday School Board. He was at that time also the director of the media center in the church where I was serving. In October of the previous year, Keith had invited me to be a featured speaker at the library/media conferences at both Ridgecrest and Glorieta. My assignment was "bibliotherapy," to address the use of books in ministering to the needs of hurting people. Keith knew that I was an avid reader and often used books in my counseling ministry. This background, he believed, qualified me for the job.

That summer of 1973 I attended both conferences and discovered something amazing. At both Glorieta and Ridgecrest there were large numbers of bright, capable, highly motivated men and women who wanted to be used in impacting lives for Jesus Christ. To be honest, I had never seen anything like what I experienced in those weeks. Certainly I had attended conferences before. Most of the time the study time was designed to be in the morning and evening. The afternoons were left free for important things like golf, shopping, or a nap. The sessions were usually excellent but one would not feel compelled to attend every occasion if there were other things that came up. After all, this was vacation. No one wanted the demands to be too heavy. Not so with media people! They had come to work, and work they did. They were being equipped for ministry and they seized every opportunity of study like they'd never have another. I came home impressed. There were few people I'd ever been exposed to in the life of the church who had this kind of zeal and enthusiasm. In the vernacular of our day, "They were ready to roll!"

In the years that have passed, some thirteen now, nothing has changed my opinion. As pastors, we have some highly qualified, deeply committed people serving with us in the church who are the Marthas of this generation. They work behind the scenes, rarely receiving the kind of recognition they deserve. But they have at their disposal key methods and the manpower to help us accomplish the task the Father has called us to do.

When Keith Mee asked me to write a book on using media in witnessing, I could not refuse. Frankly, I had never seriously considered the enormous implications of the use of media in doing the task that pastors are so vitally involved in. Like communication, we often take media for granted. It is just part of our lives like the plumbing system in our homes or the circulation system in our bodies. Until someone calls our attention to it, we rarely take notice. But when one stops to consider the multitude of ways that media can and should be used in propagating the gospel, it seems rather amazing that this book has so long gone unwritten.

My deepest hope and prayer is that the concepts shared in this book will be read and taken seriously by a great host of pastors. Beyond that, my desire is to affirm and encourage the unnoticed, unsung, and sometimes unappreciated media library workers who have for so long labored with great faithfulness for our Lord.

Together, you and I, pastor and people, are on mission. Together, we have the joy and privilege of sharing the good news of Christ. We are co-laborers. How can the eye tell the ear that it is not needed? How can any of us say to the other, "Your ministry is of lesser importance"? Surely, that would be a presumption that is incorrect. I thank God for our mutual ministry.

My deepest thanks also goes to my wife, Dwain, who is my encourager, my sweetheart, and my proofreader. Without her my infinitives would be split. Carmel Baptist Church of Charlotte, North Carolina, is the marvelous, progressive church that has allowed me to be its pastor over the past ten years. They provided me with a sabbatical so that this book might be written in the quiet of the mountain home of my mother and father-in-law, Lasca and Bill Horsley. My deepest thanks go to both the church and my wife's wonderful parents for their generosity. One final word of appreciation is due to my secretary, Mrs. Jo Barksdale, without whom much of what I accomplish would remain only something that should be done.

DON BOULDIN

Franklin, North Carolina
July 1986

Contents

Introduction

God has always used media to speak to man. He used the burning bush, writing on Belshazzar's wall, tablets written by his own finger, prophets who acted out His message, and songs sung by the singer David. Finally, the message was wrapped in human flesh. Every method carried the same message. Sinful, separated man is being pursued and provided for by a loving, caring, sacrificial God.

Media is a big word today. Our culture is message oriented. We are bombarded with thousands of messages each day, many of them geared to stimulate us to consume more of the world's goods. TV, radio, newspapers, magazines, billboards—all inform us what to buy, what products are preferred, where to eat, the price of the neighbor's house, what's on special this week, the best car on the market, where to spend our vacation. And to help us make these decisions there is a constant barrage of commercials that increasingly sound theological: "Datsun saves," "K-Mart is your saving place," "GE: We bring good things to life," "Buick, something to believe in."

None of these things, however, solves the hunger deep within modern humanity. Only the message of Jesus Christ will do that. Christians have the most powerful message in the world. The question now is how that message is best communicated. One of the many stories told on Yogi Berra illustrates the point perfectly. Someone said of the former New York Yankee Hall of Famer, "Yogi knows more baseball than all the rest of the team put together. Too bad he can't tell us about it." You see, one may possess a great message, but that isn't enough. He must also possess the ability to communicate that message. The message of Jesus Christ is the "good news" that the world is longing for, but it must be communicated and communicated well. Every form of media must be used to share that message. God's people must become adept at using the most effective means of using media to get the word out to a waiting world.

When I was growing up in central Texas, our lives were filled with colloquialisms. One old word of wisdom that jumps out in my memory is the notion, "There are many ways to skin a cat!" Translated, that means there are usually many ways to accomplish any given task. Certainly that is true with the process of sharing the gospel. Innovative Christians have hundreds of ways available to them to share the "good news" of salvation in Jesus Christ with someone who has never heard.

Sermons, songs, and signs are all tools used to propagate the message. God's good news has been spoken over the airwaves, dramatized in film, sung in great cathedrals and small country churches, and written on subway walls. In every instance media was involved. One definition of media is "a means of effecting or conveying something . . . channels of communication." Obviously that includes something as simple as a Baptist layman giving his testimony to a friend and something as sophisticated as television broadcasts via a satellite. Media is the means we use to "get out" the best news our world has ever heard.

This book is designed to stimulate your thinking. Don't allow yourself to fall into the trap of designating "media" to mean only books or tapes or any other single thing you might have in mind. Remember that media is any instrument through which the message is shared. Never has there been a day when so many forms of media were so readily accessible. All of us who love Jesus and want to tell his story would be wise to utilize media to the maximum.

So where do we begin? Maybe there is a neighbor having marriage problems who needs a book about marriage placed in her hands today. There are many such books available today.

Or it could be that no one else could speak so effectively to your friend as James Dobson. He has reached thousands by both the written and spoken word. Dobson has spoken to America about marital and family needs. Friends who would never attend your church, go to your pastor for counseling, or visit a secular psychiatrist will come to a Dobson film when it is presented in an unthreatening setting. Also, many effective speakers have made available tapes of their sermons that you can use to deal with a friend's needs. It is important for you to begin to explore the media available for your use and the way it can best be used.

Most important of all, perhaps, is Marshall McLuhan's statement "The medium is the message." You may be the most effective instrument God has to communicate the message of God's love to a lost friend. After all, that person can see in you or fail to see in you what these marvelous writers and preachers are talking about. Hopefully, these pages will also be filled with encouragement and inspiration for you to act out the good news of Christ so that others can see you up close and want your experience to be theirs.

1

Sharing the Message

Word association is interesting. Mention a certain word, and a thought or a picture pops into your mind. Let's try it. Football! How about it? What did you think of? The Chicago Bears? Beautiful fall days at your favorite college stadium? Cold, windy autumn nights when you watched a son play for his high school team? All of those pictures and more come to mind for me.

Try another one. Vacation! That could be a million things. Driving cross-country with the kids in the back of the station wagon . . . fighting all the way. The week at the beach when the whole family got together and you got a terrific sunburn. That dream vacation to Europe that you have planned for twenty years. You see what I mean about word association? Mention a word and a thousand thoughts come to mind.

Now, let's try another word. Media! When I was asked to write this book and deal with the subject of media as it relates to witnessing, some thoughts immediately came to my mind. Media! Hummm . . . ! That word brings to mind books, tapes, records, the Dewey Decimal System. It reminds me of the media library down the hall from my office. Media means all the dedicated people who work in that room checking out books, cutting tapes, seeing to it that overheads and tape players get to the right rooms on Sunday. But there is a catch here. How does all that relate to witnessing?

Interesting, isn't it, how our experiences color the meaning of words. Often we are very limited in what we think simply because we've never experienced anything else. *Media* is a term that conjures up all the images I've mentioned, but obviously it's so much more than that. So, the more I thought about it, the more it was clear that I needed a better definition. I needed to broaden my concept of what media really meant.

The "What" of Media

In the introduction I defined media as "a means of effecting or conveying something . . . channels of communication." But we need to be a bit more specific. The obvious conclusion is to see what Mr. Webster has to say. *Webster's New World Dictionary of the American Language* defines media as "any means, agency, or instrumentality; specifically, a means of communication that reaches the general public." If I use that definition and apply it to evangelism, I could easily define media in this way: "Media is any way, any instrument, any vehicle that one employs in the sharing of the gospel with the general public (lost world)."

Think of the enormous implications of that definition. Talk about broadening the concept! This means that all the things we do . . . preaching, teaching, counseling, visiting, fellowships, athletic teams, camps, retreats . . . all of it involves media. Each one of these practices or events is a method that we are utilizing to directly or indirectly get out a message.

The "Why" of Media

Once the definition is in mind, it is important to deal with another question. Why should there be a concern in the Christian community about the use of media in evangelism? Certainly there are numbers of people, particularly pastors, I might add, who see "media" as the activity confined to that little room down the hall from my office. Large numbers of our church people have in their mind that "media" has little if anything to do with witnessing. I suspect that even significant numbers of those who give much of their time to enlarging, enhancing, and equipping the media ministries in our churches have some difficulty in tying media and witnessing together. So the question naturally arises: "Why address this subject at all?"

The answer to that question should be obvious by now. We have been too narrow and provincial in our understanding of the whole concept. Often without any awareness, we have been deeply involved in the use of media in many forms of ministry. Our intention here is to call attention to that and then encourage the sharpening of our skills to utilize the instruments we have to the maximum.

The "Where" of Media

Once the "why" has been established, another question looms evident. Where do we begin? Where do we start in knowing how we best communicate this message? The answer is that we must begin with God. There is no one comparable to God himself in the ability to communicate. God has repeatedly communicated with His people since that first man was created. God is pictured in Genesis as walking and talking with man. Then God chose to use people to communicate His message. The patriarchs, the prophets, the priests and kings were all communicators of the message of God to the people.

Finally came the ultimate message. God used the "media" of human flesh to express His love when He came to the world as Jesus Christ. When this world rejected God's complete revelation in Christ, He wrote His message of love so man could always have access to it. Then He came in power. Though the Holy Spirit had always impacted the life of man externally, now He came to dwell in the believer. The Holy Spirit came to man with that same message of God's love for lost mankind. His task was conviction, clarification, assurance. When men read the objective revelation of God, the Spirit underlines in that man's mind and heart the truth of the message. We must begin with God, who is the great Communicator.

The "Who" of Media

The only message we have is Jesus! He is God's singular message to a lost world. The message had been spoken in many ways to people. It had been shared through hundreds of years but, somehow, man could not understand. The message was always the same. Man has sinned. That sin has separated the creation from the Creator. But that same loving God who gives man the freedom to rebel has taken the initiative to redeem man back to Himself. From the very moment man chose to believe the Deceiver, God has been redeeming His lost creation back to Himself. He warned the evil one what would ultimately be his lot.

"So the Lord God said to the serpent, 'Because you have done this, Cursed are you above all the livestock/and all the wild animals!/You will crawl on your belly/and you will eat dust/all the days of your life./And I will put enmity/between you and the woman,/and between your offspring and hers;/he will crush your head,/and you will strike his heel'" (Gen. 3:14-15).

The prophets declared the same message. Listen to Isaiah:

"For to us a child is born,/to us a son is given;/and the government will be upon his shoulder,/and his name will be called/'Wonderful Counselor, Mighty God,/Everlasting Father, Prince of Peace.'/Of the increase of his government and of peace/there will be no end,/upon the throne of David, and over his kingdom,/to establish it, and to uphold it/with justice and with righteousness/from this time forth and for evermore" (Isa. 9:6-7, RSV).

And again in Isaiah 53:2-6 (RSV):

"He grew up before him like a young plant,/and like a root out of dry ground;/he had no form or comeliness that we should look at him,/and no beauty that we should desire him./He was despised and rejected by men;/a man of sorrows, and acquainted with grief;/and as one from whom men hide their faces/he was despised, and we esteemed him not./Surely he has borne our griefs/and carried our sorrows;/yet we esteemed him stricken,/smitten by God, and afflicted./But he was wounded for our transgressions,/he was bruised for our iniquities;/upon him was the chastisement that made us whole,/and with his stripes we are healed./All we like sheep have gone astray;/we have turned every one to his own way;/and the Lord has laid on him/the iniquity of us all."

Jesus is the message! He is God's message in human flesh. He shared the good news both visually and verbally. His actions were observed and his words heard. And, ultimately, He declared that his followers would take his model and his message and continue to propagate the good news.

First, He sent His Son. Then He sent His Spirit. Now He sends His church, that is, us. He sends us out by His Spirit into this world to announce His Son's salvation— He worked through His Son to achieve it; He works through us to make it known.[1]

Besides bringing salvation, Christ came to make visible, to reveal, and to communicate the very essence of the invisible God.[2] Everything we have to share is wrapped up in the person of Jesus Christ.

Jesus is the "Who" of media. He is the One that the world needs to know. John, the Apostle, said that God "pitched his tent" among us so we could observe His characteristics up close (John 1:14). His desire was not only that we ourselves will be reconciled to God, but that we might become carriers of His message to those who have never heard. God knew, of course, that one cannot get excited or convey convincingly a message about a person until one has known that person himself. Simply knowing about God or his message, therefore, is inadequate. I must know the object of that message . . . Jesus Christ. Otherwise, it would be comparable to my relationship to the current President of the United States, Ronald Reagan.

I know quite a bit about Mr. Reagan. I know that he is a Californian, loves horses, was a movie star, lives in the White House. I know much about him. But I do not know him. He has never made contact with me nor I with him. If today we met on a street he would not recognize me. And if by chance he did, he would care nothing about me. We are not friends or companions. I know about him but I do not know him.

But the Savior of all the universe is quite different. He took the initiative to seek me out. As with those first disciples, he established a warm, loving, relationship with me. The Gospel of John records the kind of commitment Jesus makes to those who love Him:

"I no longer call you servants, because a servant does not know his master's business. Instead, I have called you friends, for everything that I learned from my Father I have made known to you. You did not choose me, but I chose you to go and bear fruit—fruit that will last" (John 15:15-16a).

The fruit that He would have us bear involves a consistent, positive witness to those who do not know him personally. How wonderful the love of the Father really is!

Our witness is to the fact that Jesus Christ is the God-man who is God's instrument of redemption. There is no one else qualified to do that job. C. S. Lewis was right when he said:

> I am trying here to prevent anyone saying the really foolish thing that people often say about Him: 'I'm ready to accept Jesus as a great moral teacher, but I don't accept His claim to be God.' That is the one thing we must not say. A man who was merely a man and said the sort of things Jesus said would not be a great moral teacher. He would either be a lunatic—on the level with the man who says he is a poached egg—or else he would be the Devil of Hell. You must make your choice. Either this man was, and is, the Son of God: or else a madman or something worse. You can shut Him up for a fool, you can spit at Him and kill Him as a demon; or you can fall at His feet and call Him Lord and God. But let us not come with any patronizing nonsense about His being a great human teacher. He has not left that open to us. He did not intend to.[3]

Notes

1. John R. W. Stott, *Our Guilty Silence: The Church, The Gospel, and The World* (Grand Rapids: William B. Eerdmans Publishing Company, 1969), p. 15.

2. Joseph C. Aldrich, *Life-Style Evangelism: Crossing Traditional Boundaries to Reach the Unbelieving World* (Portland, Oregon: Multnomah Press, 1981), p. 31.

3. C. S. Lewis, *Mere Christianity* (New York: Macmillan Company, 1970), pp. 40-41.

2

Tell It Often, Tell It Well

Twenty-five years ago I proposed to my wife. The scene was a chapel on the campus of the college we were attending. It was a moving moment for me. I can remember that I showed her the ring and told her that I loved her and wanted to marry her. Then I asked if she would make that same commitment to me and she responded, "Yes!" I can't ever remember being happier. We kissed, laughed, and walked hand-in-hand across that beautiful campus in the late spring. The world had never been more beautiful. I was in love!

An interesting thing happened next that has gained more significance to me as the years have passed. It wasn't long until my new fiancée said to me, "I can't wait until I tell everybody." She was talking about another moment of excitement that would come for her later when she would kiss me goodnight and walk into a room filled with her college friends who would squeal, cry, laugh, "ooh" and "aah" over the ring she now wore on her left hand. She couldn't wait to tell them her good news.

But what if no one was there? What if that evening everyone had gone out of town and she walked into a dorm that was totally void of any friends of hers to celebrate this marvelous event? Or what if no one cared? Can you imagine her making the announcement only to be greeted by indifference? Or what if no one could understand? Try to imagine the frustration of making that kind of announcement when no one caught on. They just couldn't seem to understand what she meant, why this was so important, what all her excitement was about.

Now imagine another picture. An eighteen-year-old boy goes to a revival service with his girlfriend. On a Thursday night his parents make a rare exception to the rule of "no dates on school nights" to allow him and his date to attend a youth service at their church. He is in the choir loft with the rest of the young people who have sung for the evening service when the evangelist begins to describe someone in that very service who is separated from God. The more the young man listens, the more the description matches his life. As the preacher talks, it becomes apparent to him that he is the person being described. He is lost. He has violated God. In spite of his external happiness and "having it all together," there is a war waging internally. The more the evangelist speaks, the more God works in the young man's heart.

Finally the moment of invitation comes and out of the choir loft comes this eighteen-year-old athlete to give his life as completely as he understands to Jesus Christ. Everything is wonderful! He has been made new. There is a peace inside that he's never known. He can't wait to tell his date.

On the way home he tries to share with her what has happened. But she doesn't understand. He does everything he can to explain in every way he knows how, but it doesn't seem to make sense to her.

The next day he tries again . . . this time with his buddies. But once again, little response. He has the best news in the world and he wants to tell it. But no one really hears.

Communication is characteristic of the Christian life. When God changes our lives, we must tell it. Like my fiancée who could hardly wait to tell her friends that she was getting married or the young man whose life had been radically altered by Jesus Christ, every Christian has a message he must share. But it is important to know that not everyone is as anxious to hear as we are to tell. There are times when no one listens. There are other occasions when people just don't understand.

The challenge, then, for every believer is to tell the story often and tell it well. The key to telling it well is to know the characteristics of the hearers and to share our message in ways that the message will be heard and understood. Communication . . . Jesus spoke about that when he said, "Therefore go and make disciples of all nations, baptizing them in the name of the Father and of the Son and of the Holy Spirit, and teaching them to obey everything I have commanded you" (Matt. 28:19-20).

Speak So All May Hear

When Jesus gave the fledgling church what has become known as the Great Commission, his intention was that they impact every area and aspect of the world. He wanted the good news heard by every person. Jesus said that Christians are to "go" to every segment of human life with His divine message.

Sometimes a cursory reading of Jesus' command causes one to think only of the geographical implications of this imperative. Go to "all nations." More serious thought reveals, however, that more was involved here. Jesus' intention was that every man, woman, boy, girl who ever lived would hear the gospel. "All nations" has tremendous ramifications. Our Lord had in mind our going geographically, going culturally, going intellectually. His command was to go to the people. Wherever they are in their understanding, go to them. However they understand life, go to them. Whatever their sociological, financial, educational level, see to it that they hear the good news.

Jesus went on to say, "As you go, teach them to obey everything I have commanded (taught) you." That's quite an assignment! Our Lord's command to all who belong to him is to invade our world with his message and make sure that those with whom we share really understand his message. That's where media enters the picture. You see, "we are media" and we are to use media to accomplish our given task.

Speak So All May Hear . . . and Listen

A missionary was sitting in her upstairs apartment one morning. She had just received a letter from home. No letters from home had been received for a couple of months, so it was a great delight to know that she soon would know all the news from back home. To her surprise, when she opened the letter a ten-dollar bill dropped out into her lap. And because she needed the money more than she needed the news, that brought a special pleasure. No sooner had she started to read her letter than she was distracted. A man was standing beneath her windowsill. Shabbily dressed, the stranger was moving around a post that he was leaning on.

As she watched the dirty little man, she began to think about his needs. Guilt swept over her as she thought about how well she was cared for and loved. The thought occurred to her that this man must have very little and surely he was far from home. Moved by his need, she realized that she couldn't keep this money. So she took a blank piece of paper and folded the money into it and clipped it together with a small paper clip. Then she wrote on the outside these words, "Don't Despair!" With that done, she opened the window and dropped the letter out the window as you would fly a little paper airplane. The man looked up, rather puzzled. When he opened the contents he looked up again and smiled a big, toothless grin and tipped his hat and left.

The day passed rather uneventfully and she thought through the day several times about the man. That night she prayed for him. In her note she had promised that she would pray for him. So all through the night she remembered his plight.

To her surprise the next morning she was awakened by someone vigorously knocking at her door. A friend in her apartment complex had come to tell her that someone was asking for a person who fit her description. So she got up and went downstairs. The strange-looking fellow stood outside the screen with that same toothless smile. He reached inside the screen and tossed her a roll of bills. She fumbled with the money for a minute, not really knowing how to respond. Finally she said, "What's this for?" To that he replied, "That's the sixty bucks you've got coming, lady! 'Don't Despair' paid five to one!"[1]

That apocryphal story reminds me of the average Christian trying to witness for Jesus. We sit back in our cloistered churches or classes or homes all day. Finally, we see people at our window that we haven't seen before. And we assume that they are waiting with baited breath for the message we are about to share with them. With great sincerity and with many good intentions we toss out our message. We use words like "revelation" and "repentance." We speak of "justification" and "salvation." These are tremendous theological words with marvelous implications, but often the message is garbled. The listener is thinking of something else, and the intention is lost. In the process, the message never reaches its intended destination.

Our task is to share the good news. More than that, it is our responsibility to share it in such a way that those with whom we share it will listen. Dick Innes is correct when he says: "The effective Christian communicator is one who not only understands God and His Word, but also understands people and knows the needs of his audience."[2]

Truthfully, we have not always been sensitive to those

outside our doors. In the church we talk often of evangelism, witnessing, the lost, winning people to Christ. Those words become nothing more than "code words" that indicate one is a member of the inner circle. But in many churches there is no purposed intention to do more than talk. We know the "language of Zion," but there is no real intention to put feet to our jargon.

Many examples come to mind of this dilemma. Recently a young pastor in California pointed to some of the keys that helped his mission church to grow very rapidly. In the suburbs of Los Angeles, where the secular mind-set makes church growth seem like an impossibility, this church started with only the pastor and his wife and quickly grew to a church of several hundred. His answer was that they shared the gospel in such a way that the people listened.

One of the keys, according to the Rev. Rick Warren, is a sensitivity to the life-style and world-view of our secular friends. Warren calls our attention to an interesting characteristic of many worship services. Have you ever noticed how often churches gear their services to the needs of Christians on Sunday morning in the day's primary service? Then in the evening service everything is tailored toward evangelism. An evangelistic message is preached; evangelistic songs are sung. Evangelism is the stress of the service. Only one thing is wrong. Lost people rarely come to church on Sunday evening. Certainly there are exceptions to that rule. But for the most part there are few nonbelievers who attend our Sunday evening services. Like the missionary, we tend to think that everyone is looking at life from our vantage point.

Gavin Reid, an English pastor, deals with this issue in his book *The Gagging of God.* Reid calls attention to the "crisis of a non-communicating church in a non-communicative society."[3] There was a time when Great Britain was at the forefront of the Christian movement. That

country produced Charles Spurgeon, John and Charles
Wesley, William Carey. But over the last hundred years
everything has changed. Today church attendance in
Britain has fallen to an almost unbelievable 2 percent of
the population.[4] According to Reid, the failure of the
English church to change its methods to keep up with a
changing world has undermined everything it has at-
tempted.

> As fishers of men the churches no longer await the
> arrival of shoals into their carefully built reservoirs,
> and to plan church strategy on the assumption that
> uncommitted people are going to come to meetings in
> church halls is to invite frustration after frustration. To
> assume that non-attendance at church-controlled ac-
> tivities is evidence of godlessness and "hardness of
> heart" shows a complete lack of understanding of and
> sympathy with the non-churchgoer.[5]

Reid is underlining the fact that people will not respond
to a message that seems foreign to them and has no relationship to their felt needs.

Speak So All May Hear . . . and Understand

Our task is clear. Jesus said that we are to share the good
news with all the world. We are to teach that world what
he taught those first disciples. The truth of his message is
to be spoken with sensitivity and with clarity so the world
will listen and understand.

On the surface that may seem rather simple. In practice
it is much more difficult. Scientists have identified for us
one of the reasons for that difficulty. Gary R. Collins in his
book *The Magnificent Mind* explains how complex the
mind really is.

> Tucked beneath the skull in each of our heads is a
> three-pound, jellylike mound that looks like crinkled
> putty, but is actually a collection of between 10 billion

and 100 billion neurons. Each neuron is as complex as an entire small computer, and consists of a central nerve-cell core attached to a long tail and several thousand wispy "dendrites." These dendrites reach out and make contact with other dendrites, and if we could count the number of contact points (scientists call the connecting points "synapses"), it is estimated that there may be as many as 1 quadrillion in every human brain.[6]

The human brain is unbelievably intricate. Actually scientists have discovered that there are at least two brains and, perhaps, multiple brains. For years scientists have known that the brain has two parts—a left and right "cerebral hemisphere"—that are joined together by a bundle of nerves called the corpus callosum. But it wasn't until the seventies that a group of scientists at the California Institute of Technology, under the leadership of Dr. Roger Sperry, discovered that the brain could be cut in half . . . right down the middle.

The research had been done on dogs and cats, but there was still some question about humans until an operation was finally performed by this group of surgeons to try to stop severe epilepsy seizures that could not be brought under control any other way. When the surgery was performed there were minimal side-effects and a major reduction of the seizures. That success led to a number of others. Scientists then reached some brand-new conclusions about the brain, including the fact that there are at least two brains that are not duplicates of each other, as had once been assumed. Usually the two halves of the brain work together, but when the corpus callosum is severed each brain can perform separately. Each side of the brain has specific functions that radically differ from the other side.[7]

The two-brain theory is tremendously important for the Christian communicator because of the differences that occur in one's thinking due to a particular bias toward one side of the brain or the other that each of us has. Because of genetic inheritance, family life-style, and early training, most of us prefer one side of the brain more than the other. Researchers who have studied the brain have discovered that every person has two distinct thinking processes. One is analytical and verbal. These abilities are housed in the left side of the brain. Another process is intuitive and visual. These abilities are in the brain's right hemisphere. The connector of these two sides of the brain is the corpus callosum, through which these two halves communicate.[8]

When our children were in elementary school, they loved a particular segment of work called "Show and Tell." Remember how that worked? The children of the class were invited to get together something from their own experiences that they could both "show" and "tell" the class about. Maybe a little boy found a dead grass snake on the way to school. He could bring that dead skin and describe in detail all his feelings as he saw this horrible monster just before him on the way to school. Sometimes a family had taken a trip to a faraway place. That family's little one could show the pictures of her family's vacation, describing the marvels of going to a new place and experiencing new sights. They were both showing and telling.

While our children loved that event in school, little did I realize the significance of what was happening. "Show" and "tell" was an instrument that appealed to every child in the class, regardless of whether he/she was a left- or right-brain thinker. Every child in the class favored one hemisphere over the other. Therefore, certain things appealed to one that had very little meaning for someone else.

Left-brain thinkers have certain obvious characteristics. For example, they put things into sequential, logical

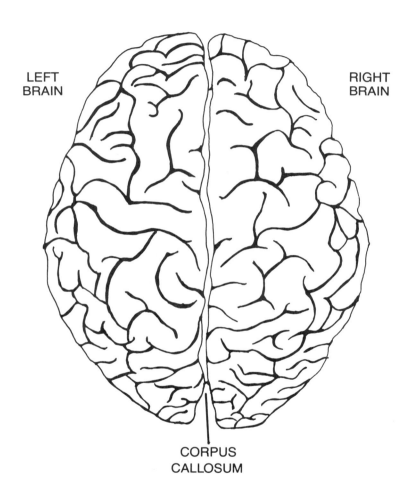

LEFT
BRAIN

RIGHT
BRAIN

CORPUS
CALLOSUM

order. (This left-brained thinking is revealed in a person's daily activities.) A person who favors his left brain will leave ten minutes early so he can drop some clothes off at the cleaners on the way to work. His left brain informs him concerning the street he should take so he can turn right into the cleaners rather than having to turn into a line of traffic with a left turn. The left brain is determined to keep one organized, sensible, and on schedule. Since this brain reads, speaks, and computes for you, it is a very vital part of your life.

Think back to your elementary school days. Did you make straight As in math, spelling, and debate? If so, you probably found it easy to memorize lists of names or dates. Adding figures came as second nature to you. You were thinking with the left hemisphere of your brain. Left-brained thinkers tend to manifest the following characteristics: positive, analytical, linear, explicit, sequential, verbal, concrete, rational, active, goal-oriented.[9]

Right-brained thinking is something quite different. If you favor the right brain you may be moved easily, take flights of fantasy, and scream at the drop of a hat. The right brain deals with the ability to appreciate and produce art, to be oriented in terms of space, to be highly creative, to be athletic, to be gifted with mechanical skills, and to enjoy anything visual.[10] The person who fantasizes about some moving experience, paints a picture, or imagines a new business idea "out of the blue" is operating in the right sphere of the brain. Characteristics of this kind of thinking include the following: intuitive, spontaneous, emotional, nonverbal, visual, artistic, holistic, playful, diffuse, symbolic, and physical.[11]

Most researchers refer to the left brain as the dominant hemisphere in our society. In turn, the right side of the brain is less dominant. Money, technology, efficiency, and power are thought to be the product of left-brain thinking. The right brain produces marvelous attributes, but our society does not prefer the mystical, intuitive, intangible, artistic values that are so prominent in some cultures. These characteristics are not as politically and socially powerful in our society as they are in many others. Other cultures or subcultures prefer right-brain thinking. This often changes, however, as an individual or group accumulates more power. Often they then acquire more of a left-brain mentality. For the most part, "successful" minority members have acquired the left-brain skills and priorities necessary to make this trip across social and financial barriers. Our society as a whole seems to consider this trip to be progress, a step from the nondominant world into the dominant.

The same kind of stress that is prevalent in the adult society dominates the thinking of our children. Think back to the time when you were in school. Do you remember the kids who could memorize long poems, calculate long lists of figures in their minds, remember history dates with ease? Remember, too, that they got high marks and praise from their parents? At the same time, in that very class there were children who wanted to look out the window and watch the rain. They would rather make up stories than conjugate verbs. These kids found it easier to create than conform. Most of the time they were in real trouble. Many gifted children learn quickly the hard and disturbing lesson that creativity tends to produce problems in their lives.

Left-brain-oriented education teaches children many important facts, but without right-brain thinking it produces very few inventors or artists. It doesn't encourage young people to be writers or composers. Thus it is important that education emphasize using both sides of the brain. Highly successful people who can deal with their own feelings as skillfully as they manage a corporation or who can raise children as wisely as they manage their own finances have usually developed a good balance between the hemispheres. It is not difficult to notice, however, that this is the minority. Most of us think with a bias toward one side of the brain or the other.

You are probably saying, "Well, all that is interesting! But what does it have to do with media? What does that say about sharing the gospel?" It has everything to do with both media and the sharing of our faith.

Our world is filled with diversity. Think of the diversity. Think of the different kinds of people that you are exposed to daily. You begin your day with your own family. In that small group there are obvious distinctions. One may gravitate to sports while another's interest is academic. One may be concerned with visual things, the way the home looks, clothes, the beauty of the surroundings. The other has a different set of interests, spending time with career, the bankbook, the practical realities of life. The children's interest varies with each child, but it's obvious that each person is different. They read different material, watch different TV programs, find different forms of media more appealing, hear different messages in the same speech. There is a wide variation of thinking and understanding even in our own homes.

Add to that the multiplicity of people you come into contact with each day. Think about the person who pumped your gas on the way to work, the secretaries in the office where you work, the one who served your meal at lunch, the young adult who checked you out at the grocery store. What about your child's coach or the teacher you recently met at PTA? Picture the mail carrier and the newspaper representative, the clothing clerk and the person who recently worked on your TV. Can you visualize the wide range of backgrounds, interests, life-styles?

Do you understand that each of these people has a particular method that would be most effective for him to receive the message of Christ? Can you see that each person thinks with either the right or the left brain and will be open to messages that appeal to his biases? Think of all the marvelous methods we have at our disposal to get that message across . . . art festivals, Bible seminars, music presentations, marriage conferences, multiple forms of recreation that develop trust and friendship. The methods we use are limited only by our imagination.

Our Lord created this magnificent mind that we have. The concept of the split brain comes as a discovery to contemporary persons, but the God of all the ages knew that some things appeal to one person while other things are more attractive to another. He created us that way. So from the beginning of God's redemptive acts He has used every form of media to say to His fallen world, "I love you!"

Notes

1. Charles R. Swindoll, Insights for Living Radio Program.

2. Dick Innes, *I Hate Witnessing* (Ventura, California: Regal Books, 1985), p. 119.

3. Gavin Reid, *The Gagging of God* (London: Hodder and Stoughton, 1969), p. 26.

4. Dick Innes, "Is Today's Church Boring?" *Encounter*, April 1972, p. 1.

5. Reid, p. 25.

6. Gary R. Collins, *The Magnificent Mind* (Waco, Texas: Word Books, 1985), p. 25.

7. Ibid., p. 28.

8. Jacquelyn Wonder and Priscilla Donovan, *Whole-Brain Thinking* (New York: Ballantine Books, 1984), p. 6.

9. Ibid., p. 3.

10. Ibid., p. 7.

11. Collins, p. 28.

3
Old Testament Models

Young people are talented these days. A high school teacher who is responsible for student government was recently describing a convention she attended where high school leaders were being trained in leadership skills. "It is unbelievable!" she said. "Those kids could speak, sing, conduct meetings, and interrelate, like they had been doing it all their lives."

That interested me. I posed the question, "Is this typical? Have young people always done this? Are these kids more talented than previous classes?"

When she answered in the affirmative to the last question, I pressed the issue. "Well, what is the difference? Why do the young people you currently work with seem to have more skills, more poise, more ability than the leaders of yesterday?"

Her response was interesting. "It's because they see all these things modeled for them. Television has an enormous impact for good and bad. One of the good things that impacts the young people of this generation is the opportunity to see and hear people who model the characteristics you've mentioned . . . skills, poise, ability to relate. They learn from what they see and hear."

No question about it! We learn from what we see and hear. Our models are important. There is no more effective way to learn something than to watch someone do it. Recently someone called my attention to the way we learn to play basketball. "We don't give a boy a copy of the rules, a basketball, and point him toward a gym. He would never learn the game that way. We take him to a place where he can see the game, feel the atmosphere, hear the sounds of the crowd. Then we place a basketball in his hand and say, 'Now, you try it.' "

How do we communicate? Tell them! Show them! The Scripture is filled with examples of that concept. God speaks both visually and verbally. Thus He appeals to the man who thinks primarily with his left brain as well as the man who is right-brained. To reach every person with a message, it must be spoken. It must also be modeled.

Old Testament messengers understood that concept. Think of the seventeenth chapter of Genesis when God chose Abram to be His man. This man would become the "Father of the Nations."

"When Abram was ninety-nine years old, the Lord appeared to him and said, 'I am God Almighty; walk before me and be blameless. I will confirm my covenant between me and you and will greatly increase your numbers.' Abram fell facedown, and God said to him, 'As for me, this is my covenant with you: You will be the father of many nations. No longer will you be called Abram; your name will be Abraham, for I have made you a father of many nations. I will make you very fruitful; I will make nations of you, and kings will come from you. I will establish my covenant as an everlasting covenant between me and you and your descendants after you for the generations to come, to be your God and the God of your descendants after you. The whole land of Canaan, where you are now an alien, I will give as an everlasting possession to you and your descendants after you; and I will be their God' " (Gen. 17:1-8).

God spoke His covenant. But God did more than that. He showed it as well. Genesis 17:9 says:

"Then God said to Abraham, 'As for you, you must keep

my covenant, you and your descendants after you for the generations to come. This is my covenant with you and your descendants after you, the covenant you are to keep: Every male among you shall be circumcised. You are to undergo circumcision, and it will be the sign of the covenant between you and me.' "

Verbal and visual. God tells his people the good news and He shows them so there can be no mistake. Everyone must understand.

Over and over again, throughout all of Scripture, God revealed himself through various media. He spoke His message and He showed it . . . through dreams, plagues, burning bushes, tablets of stone. God used the media of that day to speak to His people in a way they would understand.

Situational Messages

The Old Testament is the revelation of God at work in the life of a people. His messages are to His chosen nation. More is involved than simply the touching of a human heart by the Spirit of God. A nation needs to see God at work and hear His message for them. So God often uses situations that modify the course of history for that people to point out to them both verbally and visually His intentions for the nation He's chosen as His redemptive instrument.

Multiple examples occur from the earliest moments of recorded history. Think of Joseph in the prison cell. The visual God used in that instance was a dream. Joseph's companions, the cupbearer and the baker, had dreams that only the son of Jacob could interpret. Pharaoh would soon experience God's visual aids as well. Genesis tells us:

"When two full years had passed, Pharaoh had a dream: He was standing by the Nile, when out of the river there came up seven cows, sleek and fat, and they grazed among the reeds. After them, seven other cows, ugly and gaunt, came up out of the Nile and stood beside those on the riverbank. And the cows that were ugly and gaunt ate up the seven sleek, fat cows" (Gen. 41:1-4).

As the dream continues, Pharaoh has pictured for him the things that are about to happen to his nation. The Scripture says, "In the morning his mind was troubled" (Gen. 41:8). The ruler needed words with his pictures to understand the message. God had already chosen the narrator for this production. Joseph was standing ready. No one else had the message God had planned for Pharaoh.

"So he [Pharaoh] sent for all the magicians and wise men of Egypt. Pharaoh told them his dreams, but no one could interpret them for him. Then the chief cupbearer said to Pharaoh, 'Today I am reminded of my shortcomings. Pharaoh was once angry with his servants, and he imprisoned me and the chief baker in the house of the captain of the guard. Each of us had a dream the same night, and each dream had a meaning of its own. Now a young Hebrew was there with us, a servant of the captain of the guard. We told him our dreams, and he interpreted them for us, giving each man the interpretation of his dream' . . . So Pharaoh sent for Joseph" (Gen. 41:8b-12,14).

When words and pictures were linked together, the whole of Hebrew history was changed. God used the situation. He used visual and verbal messages to accomplish His purpose and speak so man could hear.

Few examples of God's use of sight and sound to convey His message are more pointed than Moses' experience with a bush that would not burn up. Do you remember the story? The second chapter of Exodus tells us that Moses had killed an Egyptian in a moment of anger and had run away from his world. Forty years later God was still teaching Moses lessons. He was using media. All kinds of media . . . that still small voice, the impact of a father-in-law, a burning bush.

Imagine what Moses must have felt. That day was just

another day. Nothing special. No rock slide, no cloud formations, no trumpet blasts. Just another day with the sheep. But while Moses was checking out the landscape to try to locate breakfast for his flock, an unbelievable thing occurred. Exodus 3:2-3 says:

"The angel of the Lord appeared to him in flames of fire from within a bush. Moses saw that though the bush was on fire it did not burn up. So Moses thought, 'I will go over and see this strange sight—why the bush does not burn up.' "

It is interesting that God's choice of a visual for this illustration was something very familiar. There must have been thousands, hundreds of thousands of the bushes that the Hebrew language terms "thorny shrub" in that area. There was, however, one thing different about this bush. In that area of the world these bushes often burn for no apparent reason. But they don't burn without being consumed. When Moses saw that was the case here, it really got his attention.

The burning bush, God's unique visual, prepared Moses to hear the message that the Lord intended to use a guy with a speech problem to be His spokesman. That message changed the history of the world.

The history of the Hebrews is filled with illustrations. God used sight and sound to make sure the message was heard correctly. Judges 6:1 to 8:35 says God spoke to Gideon and assured him that Gideon would be His primary instrument to save Israel. But God's voice wasn't adequate for Gideon. He wanted a visual as well. Gideon was one who demanded "Show me!" So God did that too. He answered Gideon's prayer affirmatively.

"Then Gideon said to God, 'Do not be angry with me. Let me make just one more request. Allow me one more test with the fleece. This time make the fleece dry and the ground covered with dew.' That night God did so. Only the fleece was dry; all the ground was covered with dew" (Judg. 6:39).

Interestingly, we find that Hebrew history has two models with multiple examples for each. One is the model of God relaying the message He wished to communicate with verbals and visuals. The other is God using a man or a woman to communicate that message using similar techniques.

Prophetic Messages

The messages of the prophets took on that same flavor. They were both verbal and visual so every man could understand. In Jeremiah 32 we learn that God instructed Jeremiah to buy a field. When the prophet didn't understand, God told him that he was to buy a field so that those who needed to hear God's message could see it. They could see through the purchase of that land that the day was coming when God would redeem His land. The people of God would return to that land. It was a message that anyone with ears and eyes could understand.

Nowhere could this be better illustrated than in Ezekiel 12:1-6:

"The word of the Lord came to me: 'Son of man, you are living among a rebellious people. They have eyes to see but do not see and ears to hear but do not hear, for they are a rebellious people. Therefore, son of man, pack your belongings for exile and in the daytime, as they watch, set out and go from where you are to another place. Perhaps they will understand, though they are a rebellious house. During the daytime, while they watch, bring out your belongings packed for exile. Then in the evening, while they are watching, go out like those who go into exile. While they watch, dig through the wall and take your belongings out through it. Put them on your shoulder as they are watching and carry them out at dusk.

Cover your face so that you cannot see the land, for I have made you a sign to the house of Israel.' "

Do you see it? Do you see the various forms of media that the Father used to get the attention of those who were a rebellious people? He used the verbal and the visual to ensure that everyone heard the message. He appealed to the logic, the order, the rational thinking of the left-brained thinker. At the same time, he drew the picture, he stimulated the imagination, he dramatized the truth for the one who would look at life through the impulses of the right brain. His message is for all the people.

And the Father modeled his message. He used people who could show us how to do it. His revelation is packed with examples of the way to go about getting out His Word. We look to the Old Testament, and the heroes of the faith model it for us. We see God showing them how; and, in turn, they walk us through the methods that are most effective.

God's methods are obvious with the principles of the Old Testament. (But, if you think that is clear, you "ain't seen nothin' yet.") Now let's look at Jesus.

4
God's Best Message

God has spoken to men in multiple ways. No way, however, is comparable to God's message found in the life of Jesus Christ. The Father could conceivably have used an infinite variety of methods to deliver His message finally and completely. He chose to send His Son.

Someone has compared His sending Jesus to a father whose children were in the United States, far away from their Australian home. Soon after they reached their destination they found themselves in deep trouble and wrote home for help. Quickly the father sent them letters filled with helpful instructions. When that didn't work, he wrote out guidelines that they were to live by that would keep them from doing further damage to themselves. But they disobeyed the laws. He sent messengers who told them how to live, what their father wanted, strongly encouraged reform and renewal of a right relationship with their dad. But that too failed.

Finally, there were only two options. This father could forsake his children, write them off as a failure, claim they were disobedient, ungrateful children that were never really part of him. Or he could come himself and get involved in their hurt, their sin, their failure.

While it may seem rather simplistic to compare God to that father, in a very real sense, that was exactly the position the Father found Himself in. He could write off His lost, sinful, disobedient children. Or He could come and identify with them in their lostness, their sinfulness, their disobedience. The Father chose the latter:

"The Word became flesh and lived for a while among us. We have seen his glory, the glory of the one and only Son, who came from the Father, full of grace and truth" (John 1:14).

Then Paul, in his great Christological statement, said:

"He is the image of the invisible God, the firstborn over all creation. For by him all things were created: things in heaven and on earth, visible and invisible, whether thrones or powers or rulers or authorities; all things were created by him and for him. He is before all things, and in him all things hold together. . . . For God was pleased to have all his fullness dwell in him, and through him to reconcile to himself all things, whether things on earth or things in heaven, by making peace through his blood, shed on the cross" (Col. 1:15-17,19-20).

God revealed Himself to man incarnationally. He wrapped Himself in human flesh. The father came to the wayward, sinful child and identified completely with his hurts and problems. Then to ensure that the child understood the message of love, God taught that child with messages that were once again verbal and visual. Think of the multiplicity of times that Jesus used visual aids that He could either point to and say, "Look, see that! The kingdom of God is like that!" or He could say, "Do you remember what a mustard seed is like?" and the listener would conjure up in his mind a visual image of something that was familiar and clear to him. Thus our Lord's message was clear to both the right- and left-brain thinker. The ultimate Media consistently used the media available to Him to communicate the message.

The fourth chapter of Mark is a prime example of the way Jesus focused the attention of His listeners on the message He wished to convey. The Scripture says that Jesus was being followed by a crowd so large that He could not adequately address them all without using the media that was available. So He gathered them together on the shore and He pushed out in a boat into the water and began to address the crowd.

"On another occasion Jesus began to teach by the lake. The crowd that gathered around him was so large that he got into a boat and sat in it out on the lake, while all the people were along the shore at the water's edge" (Mark 4:1).

Is it possible that Jesus took advantage of one of nature's methods of communication there? Since the human voice is limited in its volume and ability to speak to massive crowds, Jesus may have simply used the water that was available to reflect his voice so it was heard by that capacity crowd. One can hardly imagine Jesus shouting until his voice was hoarse and tired. Instead, he probably sat quietly and, in the manner of the teacher of his day, taught a massive crowd with the help of nature's built-in media.

Notice too the way he taught. Once again he used both the verbal and the visual to make his point. Mark 4:3 says, "Listen! A farmer went out to sow his seed." Can you imagine that there on the hillside of the beautiful hills that surround the Sea of Galilee, the farmers were busy doing what they did daily at certain times of the year . . . sowing seeds. Certainly if there were no farmers there on the day our Lord told the story, there was not one in the crowd who had not seen that picture hundreds of times before. So Jesus used the media available to him to teach the lessons of faith.

One only has to begin to read the Gospels to see Jesus appear as the unrivaled teller of tales. He realized, of course, that adults are simply children "grown up" and that little child in all of us always wants to be around someone who will "tell us a story." So, stories He told. We call them parables. And with each parable He told came a picture. He used mental imagery and the human voice to take some familiar object or scene and from it derive a spiritual truth.

When we read the stories of Jesus we can almost smell the baking of the bread and see a woman patching the garments. We can visualize the emergency that precipitated a friend's borrowing a loaf of bread at midnight for his sudden guests. Poor homes and rich mansions alike are etched in our mind's eye as we hear the Master talk. Can't you see barns bursting with fatness, workers not daring to eat until their master had broken his fast, selfish men scrambling for seats of authority and power?

Jesus, the master communicator, had the ability to use every media resource available to picture the whole gamut of human experience . . . farmers plowing in their fields, fishermen struggling with both empty and bulging nets, a wedding procession moving through the dark with flickering torches, kings marching off to war, the widow whose single mite made a more significant sound in the treasury than the clank of coins deposited by the rich. It's all in the stories He told.

We see fields "white unto harvest," and hillsides where the faithful shepherd beds down his sheep for the night. Off in the distance in that same picture is the vineyard on a favored slope, or a dark valley where brigands lurk. Jesus, the divine painter of pictures and teller of stories, made it easy in His style of communication to understand the central message of his life: God loves this world enough to come Himself in human flesh.

Sometimes we have been slow to pick up on the model Christ provided for us. The contemporary proclaimer of the good news too often seems content to use only one method or, perhaps, a few methods to propagate the message rather than using every method available to get out the Word. Then that same proclaimer is often puzzled by the lack of response to the message. What preacher hasn't been frustrated and occasionally angered by the apparent indifference that some in the congregation manifest when he has faithfully spoken the gospel message? Why, there are people in that congregation who actually doze while he is preaching!

I'll never forget a particular fellow who always sat on the front row of a church in Mississippi. He apparently went to sleep the moment I got up to preach. One Monday morning I ran into him and decided to ask him about his sleeping practices in church. "Mr. Herbert," I quizzed, "how did you like the morning message yesterday?"

"Oh, it was a dandy, preacher," he declared.

Amused, I pushed on. "Well, tell me, what was the point that really stuck in your mind?"

At that point he proceeded to tell me several things in the sermon that were meaningful to him. When he finished, I was a bit embarrassed and confessed to him that I had intended to shame him for going to sleep in church and now I was ashamed myself for suspecting something that obviously was not true. He laughed and said, "Oh no, Preacher, I'm not sleeping in church. I'm just resting my eyes." Far too many of us have people in church with their eyes shut. Maybe, like Mr. Herbert, they are just resting their eyes. But more than likely, they are asleep. Count on it! Those folks will never hear the message. It is not being communicated.

Communicators often seem surprised when a "sleeper" in the crowd suddenly wakes up when only moments before he seemed so bored. If one took the time to notice, that same sleeper may be the very one sitting on the edge of his seat and soaking it all up when something visual is presented. Should the choir do something with beautiful visual aids accompanying their singing, this fellow comes alive. He's all ears . . . or, perhaps better said, he's all eyes. When that kind of situation occurs, the chances are good that the man under discussion is a right-brain thinker who will rarely be reached effectively with the message of the gospel by methods that appeal primarily to the left-brain thinker.

Charles H. Kraft, in his book *Communication Theory for Christian Witness*, points out some interesting and important concepts. He says that when one thinks of "proclaiming" the gospel, the practice of preaching immediately comes to mind.

> The custom of preaching represents the church's adoption of Greek oratorical practice as the central focus of its communicational activity. Though the use of such oratory in church contexts has been common since early times, it was apparently during the Reformation that Protestants replaced the mass with a monologue lecture (the sermon) as the central feature of the worship service. The present place and nature of monologue homilies in Protestant worship are thus relatively recent origin.[1]

To say that anything other than the proclaimed Word is primary in Christian worship goes contrary to who we are and what we believe as Christians. But before we react, maybe we'd better look at the meaning of that word the New Testament used for "proclamation" and how it was applied in the early church. The Greek word *kerusso* (and its derivatives) was the popular word used to describe the proclamation of the gospel. Like many other New Testament words, it did not originally cover every kind of activity to which it later was applied. *Kerusso* originally referred mainly to the announcing that the town criers did as they moved from house to house and from town to town, making some kind of important announcement that the populace needed to hear. They were sharing the news in much the same fashion that it is shared via radio and television today. Kraft insists:

> The word was chosen by early Christians and used in an expanded way to refer to a much wider range of

communicational activity. It included a monologue lecturing but was also used to label interactions that were mainly dialogical, as long as the focus was on the communication of the gospel. It is interesting confirmation of this fact that John, perhaps sensing the limitations of this word, consistently uses the word witness (martureo) in its place.[2]

Kraft insists that while the word could be correctly translated "proclaim," an even better translation for contemporary English might be "communicate." The task of the Christian is to communicate the gospel.

Our model is Jesus Christ, the master communicator. We must use his pattern. To do that, our communication must be incarnational. The lost man must both see and hear in our lives the message of salvation. Beyond that it is our responsibility to utilize every method, every media that is at our disposal to communicate our message. Our day is an exceptional one. We have at our disposal technology that our forefathers never dreamed about. Communication techniques that appeal both to the verbal and the visual are available to us and it is our responsibility to use them. We cannot be content to use one or two. The familiar is not necessarily the best. Certainly it isn't the best for all who need to hear or, perhaps, see God's Word.

Notes

1. Charles H. Kraft, *Communication Theory for Christian Witness* (Nashville: Abingdon Press, 1983), p. 43.
2. Ibid.

5
Jesus, the Master Communicator

Clyde Reid introduces his book *The Empty Pulpit* with the story of "The Complacent Sower." In the modern-day parable he pictures a farmer who is extremely naive about his task.

> One fine morning a farmer set out to plant his field. He walked up and down with his seed bag at his waist, throwing the seed in a rhythmic motion with his head held high. He would feel the warm sun on his face as he walked. "I love to watch the blue skies and the gentle clouds as I plant," he said to himself. "As I sow, I can dream of the great harvest to come. I can imagine the hungry children this crop will feed. I can see the workers who will earn their bread by the fruits of my labor. Surely, this is God's work!" Finally satisfied he had sown enough, he went back to the farmhouse to think and wait. And the rains came and the sun shone on that field.
>
> One week later, the farmer went again to his field and again he sowed a great deal of seed, walking up and down sowing to right and to left with his head held high looking at the clouds. Again he returned satisfied. "Surely, this is God's work," he murmured to himself. The other six days he spent sorting over his seed and studying the seed catalogues.
>
> Again the next week, and every week that followed, he did the same, sowing great quantities of seed, then returning to the farmhouse to await the results.[1]

As the parable develops, one can almost anticipate the conclusion. The farmer continues to plan and dream. But when harvesttime comes and the farmer is anticipating a tremendous in-gathering, he is bitterly disappointed. The fields are barren.

Angry and confused, the farmer goes to experts who can advise him where he had made his mistakes. One consultant says, "Well, it is obvious that you did not prepare the ground before planting. The earth was not plowed for seed, so it simply lay on top of the hard ground and did not put down roots."

A second expert advised that the farmer had sown too much seed and the seeds had choked out each other. Still a third adviser came forth with the conclusion that one man had tried to do the work of many. "Could you not train a crew of fellow workers to labor with you?"[2]

But the parable says that the farmer paid no heed to the advice of the experts. The next sowing season he was at it again, sowing, sowing, more sowing. Someone asked him why he did not heed the good advice he was given. His reply was, "Oh, those fellows! I'm sure they meant well. But not one of them is a farmer. Why should I listen to them? You can't tell me there will be no harvest. That is in God's hands alone, and His standards are not our standards. His ways are not our ways. Besides, I enjoy standing out here once a week in the warm sun with my head high sowing this seed. To be a farmer is to be a sower of seed. I find my occupation rewarding."[3]

The farmer, the conclusion of the parable instructs, went on with that process year after year while his friends shook their heads in amazement.

Reid's parable is pointed! It takes little imagination to realize that many of us who are trying to communicate the gospel effectively somehow seem to find ourselves in the plight of the naïve, complacent sower. The parable was directed primarily toward the preacher of the good news who stands in the pulpit week after week, sowing those seeds of the gospel, but has little concern over the results of his labors. But one must not stop with the preacher. The same kind of thing could be said of the teacher, the Church Training leader, the youth worker. It could be said of the media library worker who faithfully catalogs media and decorates the promotion window.

This could not be said of Jesus! Jesus was the most effective communicator who ever lived. His message, His deeds, His methods, His life—all communicated. When He communicated, He upset the religious leaders, but the masses of common people heard Him with great joy.

When Jesus communicated he didn't use an ad on TV or an article in the paper to relay His message; but His methods were contemporary. He used the language that the people understood. He spoke in a way that captured the hearts and minds of His listeners, and He used every method available. Then Jesus invented some new methods of His own. He painted pictures with words. He wrote in the sand, answered questions with questions, enlisted the authority of Scripture. He did it all. And people from every culture, every socioeconomic background, heard Him.

Wherever Jesus went, He communicated. He said to people, "God loves you!" The paralyzed man Jesus healed heard that. So did the publican He enlisted, the ruler's daughter He restored to life. When He opened the eyes of the blind and cured the diseases of the hurting, when He raised Lazarus, and when the possessed was set free, they all heard the message. Jesus is the master communicator.

At this point we must not be like the sower of seed who hears of a better way. He sees a model that, if followed, would produce better results. But he refuses to listen. We must not make that mistake. Instead, we need to seek out the example of life's premier communicator. Since God has called us to be communicators, let's compare our way to the perfect model, Jesus Christ.

Ralph Lewis raises an interesting question for communicators when he asks, "Is everyone as eager to hear your sermon as you are to preach it? Or are there built-in barriers for even the best-built, most creatively constructed sermon?"[4] He answers that question by citing some interesting discoveries of modern science. "When we preach today," Lewis says, "we face the challenge of the triple brain. We've all heard much in recent years about right and left brain but what is this about a triple brain? Current literature discusses the three levels of the human brain as R-complex, the limbic system, and the cerebrum."[5]

If the brain is broken down into the categories of modern science some very interesting discoveries are made that relate to communication. The R-complex or brain stem produces our instinctual behavior. For instance, it is this part of the brain that tells us to shorten our breaths and keep our hands and arms close to our bodies when we encounter someone who causes us to be alarmed. The primary concern of the R-complex part of the brain is our own personal comfort. Science tells us that a snake has only an R-complex brain, and it will find the warmer rock even if the temperature only varies 1/1000th of a degree. That same scientist will insist that every one of us has an innate drive for personal comfort. Both personal experience and the evaluation of others confirm that notion.[6]

What does this mean to the communicator? It means that we must be concerned with the comfort zones of each individual listening to the message we are trying to share. Harsh, threatening words may get someone's attention but may block the message. There is a fine line between sustaining interest and alienating. Once again, Jesus was the master. Picture His approach as He spoke to the Samaritan woman in the fourth chapter of John.

"When a Samaritan woman came to draw water, Jesus said to her, 'Will you give me a drink?' " (John 4:7). The reaction of the woman tells us that his question was just right to enlarge her comfort zone adequately so that a meaningful conversation could ensue. "The Samaritan woman said to him, 'You are a Jew and I am a Samaritan woman. How can you ask me for a drink?' (For Jews do not associate with Samaritans)" (v. 9).

The barriers went down! Jews did not speak to Samaritans. Neither did they speak to women in public. But Jesus did. And he did so in such a way that the defenses came down and the woman could hear the message of salvation. Jesus got her attention. But he did not alienate her in the process.

Nicodemus was another person whom Jesus impacted because of his ability to walk that narrow line between getting attention and alienation. After all, the things Jesus said to Nicodemus were not easy to understand or accept. "You must be born again!" Are you kidding? What does that mean? "Talk sense!" Nicodemus might have said. But Jesus, with His marvelous sensitivity to people, was able to appeal to the R-Complex segment of the mind with every person He encountered. An interesting study for all of us who are trying to give our faith away in the most effective way possible would be to study the multiple scriptural examples and to evaluate the way Jesus was able to do just that.

Lewis, in his article, mentions another segment of the brain that is also important to the communicator. The limbic system or "visceral brain" is that part which "responds to the feeling level" of those things we share. No communicator needs to be told that people who hear the message are deeply impacted by their feelings. What may come as a surprise is the sensitivity with which Jesus handled those feelings. "Come to me, all you who are weary and burdened," He said, "and I will give you rest" (Matt.

11:28). "The emotional level rises in these feelings of the words of Jesus. Where is their logical appeal? You'll find none. Here the appeal is to feeling—universal feelings, rather than to intellect."[7]

Far too often the Christian communicator's appeal lacks the emotional content that is needed. Our pattern is too often modeled after educators in the public arena who devote as much as 85 to 90 percent of their time and energy trying to develop the cognitive area of our lives. They forget somehow that 40 to 50 percent of our lives is impacted primarily by our emotions.

Not so with Jesus. He knew two millenniums ago what modern educators are just discovering. Ivy League researchers a few years ago picked up on the idea that emotional appeals are mainly centered around two emotions: promises and fear. The scientists insisted that their research proved that optimists respond more to promises while pessimists react more to threats. An interesting observation is that Jesus' longest sermon was based on that same premise. Approximately 60 percent of the message that we call the Sermon on the Mount was faith-promises. About 40 percent of that message was implied fear-threats. Jesus understood that in every group there are people who respond positively to both categories. So when he spoke, he appealed to the primary emotions of our lives.

Lewis makes an interesting point.

> The experts say the average American faces 600 emotional appeals each week. Every member of the congregation said 'No' to 590 appeals for action before coming to church. Now they're primed to say 'No' to your message as well.[8]

We need to know that. It underlines the fact that every message we share must have magnetic emotional content. It must be designed to appeal to the emotions in the same way that Jesus appealed to that important segment of humanity's personality.

Still a third segment of the brain must be mentioned. The cerebrum is the highest level of the brain. This is the part of the brain that we have mentioned as actually being divided into the right and left brain. Once again, Jesus was sensitive to this phenomenon as well as the other aspects of the human mind that we've discussed. Would it surprise you to discover that Jesus often accented his appeal to the person who was primarily right-brained? Jesus' messages were primarily narrative in nature. He related experiences, shared deep feelings, used many comparisons, and often told stories of everyday life. Jesus' approach is exactly the opposite of the way preaching is most often taught in the seminaries of today. The approach today seems to highlight the cognitive, while Jesus' messages focused on the emotions.

Jesus was indeed the Master Communicator. And it is the need of every Christian to follow the example of Jesus. He should be our model as we try to give away the good news. We should look to Jesus for the methods as well as the message. And when we do, we see clearly that Jesus knew all the latest methods before humans ever even began to think about them. He spoke to every listener in a way uniquely designed for the way God had put that person together. When Jesus spoke, the people listened. And they received life.

Notes

1. Clyde Reid, *The Empty Pulpit* (New York: Harper and Row Publishers, 1967), pp. 13-14.

2. Ibid., p. 14.

3. Ibid.

4. Ralph Lewis, "The Triple Brain Test of a Sermon," *Preaching,* September/October 1985, p. 9.

5. Ibid.

6. Ibid.

7. Ibid., p. 10.

8. Ibid.

6
Communication Is the Name of the Game

A story told on a well-known pastor may have been true. It seems that back in the days of the Jesus revolution, in the late sixties, the pastor had a long-haired, "Jesus music" group come to his church to lead in a youth worship service on a Sunday evening.

A number of older members were in that particular service that evening and were very displeased by what took place. The pastor really wasn't too surprised by that. But he was also very aware that the young people in the service thought everything that happened was terrific.

At the close of the service, the pastor was standing at the back door, greeting the parishioners as they left to go home. An older lady approached him with a sour look on her face. "Brother John," she began, "I want you to know how disappointed I am that you allowed that straggly-haired, unkempt, dirty bunch to sing in our service this evening. I thought they were just terrible and all my friends felt exactly that way too." The pastor smiled and nodded. Then he said, "Well, Mrs. Brown, I understand your concern. But let me tell you about a philosophy that seems appropriate for this kind of occasion. For years," he continued, "when I went fishing I would take ham sandwiches and I would take worms. The ham sandwiches were for me, not the fish. Think about that a while and apply the principle to this evening's meeting."

The story may be apocryphal. Or it may have happened. Nevertheless, it illustrates well a very valid concept for all of us who are in the business of sharing our faith. If one is to be effective in sharing the message, communication is the name of the game. And in order to get the message across, the communicator must begin where that person hearing the message happens to be at this particular moment. When you go fishing, you may prefer ham sandwiches, but the catch of the day only bites when you offer him worms.

James F. Engel and H. Wilbert Norton in their book *What's Gone Wrong with the Harvest? A Communication Strategy for the Church and World Evangelism* indicate that most churches are trying their best to communicate the message of Christ. But many of those churches would have to admit that there is still something to be desired in the results they are having.

An amazing statement was recently made in a large gathering of Southern Baptists in one of the most successful Baptist states. The chairman of evangelism of that particular convention reported to a number of concerned pastors, "Gentlemen, at the current time, we are not even baptizing our own children." What's wrong? There are hundreds, even thousands of Bible-believing, Bible-preaching and teaching churches who would have to admit that was the case in their own congregations. The question that Engle and Norton posed in *What's Gone Wrong with the Harvest?* is pertinent for this hour.

The professors did not simply pose a question; however, they also proceeded to give some clear-cut answers. Their conviction is that much of the answer lies in the area of communication. Simply verbalizing the message is not enough, they say. In order for decisions to be made, lives to be changed, that message must be heard, appropriated, and integrated into the life-style of the hearer.

The question naturally arises, "How does the Christian communicator go about seeing that this is happening in his own ministry?" Engle and Norton insist that our Lord himself has given us some distinctive answers, a biblical pattern, that if followed would virtually solve much of the dilemma we currently struggle with.[1]

Jesus and His disciples provide ideal models for contemporary communicators. The pattern they used might be outlined as follows:[2]

1. They Understood Their Audience

Jesus was nobody's fool. He understood the heart and mind of mankind. Over and over in Scripture He illustrated this. When a teacher of Israel, Nicodemus, came to Jesus at night and asked that Jesus help him solve the age-old problem of man, separation from God, Jesus knew his heart. He understood, as they say in today's vernacular, "where he was coming from." Jesus told him that reform and good works weren't adequate to solve his problem. He needed to be re-created. But Nicodemus balked. That was something new to him and he couldn't understand that concept at all.

" 'You are Israel's teacher,' said Jesus, 'and do you not understand these things? I tell you the truth, we speak of what we know, and we testify to what we have seen, but still you people do not accept our testimony. I have spoken to you of earthly things and you do not believe; how then will you believe if I speak of heavenly things? No one has ever gone into heaven except the one who came from heaven—the Son of Man. Just as Moses lifted up the snake in the desert, so the Son of Man must be lifted up, that everyone who believes in him may have eternal life' " (John 3:10-14, NIV).

Jesus understood Nicodemus. He also understood Nicodemus' forefathers. The Lord realized that there was something missing at the core of their lives. When God led Nicodemus' spiritual forefathers through the wilderness, they didn't like the way they were led. They didn't like the way they were fed. And God punished them because their hearts were selfish and wicked. He raised up serpents to bite them and bring death. But he also brought a Redeemer. When the bronze serpent was lifted up in that wilderness, rebellious lives that were doomed were redeemed (Num. 21:4-9). Jesus knew the basic nature of those who heard his message. He knew their rebellious heart. He knew their selfish spirit. And He knew that there was in their lives a character flaw that nothing but re-creation could change.

Nicodemus' problem, of course, began just like modern humanity's. It began when that first man willfully disobeyed God and broke the relationship that was perfect. Once that was done, self-serving became Adam's life-pattern. That same life-style has been passed on to spiritual descendants and has not changed in all the history of mankind. Persons are incomplete. Our destiny is to live with everything in life being filtered through our desire to please ourselves. While we know that there must be something beyond and better than what we now experience, life is colored continually by our own selfishness.

The problem of selfishness is the consistent reality that Jesus had to deal with as He addressed the audiences who heard Him speak. It is the problem that colors everything that is heard when the gospel is presented today. The self-centeredness prevalent in every heart serves as a filter to prohibit any message from penetrating into a life unless the message is one the hearer desires to hear.

Talk all you want about God and Jesus. Your talk falls on deaf ears unless the hearer identifies that message as something pertinent and meaningful to his life. The selfishness spoken of earlier filters out the message until it fails to penetrate the needy heart. That will be illustrated further in a later chapter.

2. They Adapted to Their Audience

Read the messages of Jesus, His disciples, and the apostle Paul, and the same conclusion will be reached. They spoke to the needs of that particular audience. To fishermen Jesus said, "I will make you fishers of men." The Samaritan woman was amazed when Jesus asked her for a drink. When her interest was keenly aroused He said to her, "If you knew the gift of God and who it is that asks you for a drink, you would have asked him and he would have given you living water" (John 4:10). That led to a conversation where Jesus revealed an acute awareness of her needs. In turn, she let down those barriers; she took away the filters that would have prohibited her hearing and listened to the message of redemption that Jesus would share with her.

The message of Jesus and His followers varied continually. This does not mean that they violated in any way the original intent of that message. They simply understood the audience. Jesus adapted his message to the needs of the people to whom He spoke. Think of the word Jesus spoke to Mary and Martha when they came in sorrow to the Master after the death of their brother, Lazarus. He could have said, "Buck up, sisters, I'm going to take care of this!" When they began their rather angry accusations concerning his failure to come when they called, He could have replied, "You don't know what you are talking about! Just wait until I raise him from the grave and you'll be sorry you acted this way." Instead He took this moment of need to tell them something they would understand completely in days to come.

"I am the resurrection and the life. He who believes in me will live, even though he dies; and whoever lives and believes in me will never die. Do you believe this?" (John 11:25).

Paul, the apostle, used the same kind of approach as did

Jesus. The issue of the moment, the mood of the audience, and the crisis or concern that impacted the lives of those who heard was the cue for the message. When Paul wrote the Corinthians, he dealt with a church divided. Why? That was their concern. They were caught up in it and probably could not see the harm and damage it was doing. So the apostle spoke directly.

"My brothers, some from Chloe's household have informed me that there are quarrels among you. What I mean is this: One of you says, 'I follow Paul'; another, 'I follow Apollos'; another, 'I follow Cephas'; still another, 'I follow Christ.' Is Christ divided? Was Paul crucified for you? Were you baptized into the name of Paul?" (1 Cor. 1:11-13).

That was the occasion that Paul used to teach the Corinthians something about the need of God's people to be one in Christ. Notice that he used concrete material. There was nothing abstract about this. "Chloe's household have informed me." Paul understood the situation. He spoke to the needs of the hour. Naturally his message was pertinent and relevant. The result was open ears, defenses down, message heard.

Who's Got the Key?

The picture is clear. Christians have been charged with the responsibility of sharing the marvelous message of Christ. We are, for the most part, serious about the task. Many of us have been working for years to try to do exactly that, but we are often frustrated because no matter how often we throw out the message, the object of that attempt never seems to hear. Now we discover that we haven't been too sharp in the way we are going about our work. Most of us have never even thought seriously about the biblical patterns of communication.

Sometimes, without even being aware of what we are doing, we have sized up our audience and adapted our

methods, but most of the time we have just used traditional methods and thrown out the message, "Don't despair!"
We justify that kind of evangelism by quoting Isaiah 55:
11, which says that God's Word will not return to Him
void. Many of us have quoted that at one time or another
and then explained that we need not worry about how the
gospel is presented. We just need to be faithful to get out
the message, and He will do the rest. Unfortunately, that's
not the meaning of that passage at all. This passage
"makes reference to the great promises God has given
Israel, especially those to be fulfilled after the return of
the Messiah. It asserts that God stands behind His cove-
nants, and the purpose was to give comfort."[3]

Most of the time we use that passage out of context.
When we were seminarians in New Orleans, it was our
practice to go every Thursday evening and preach on the
street corner in the old French Quarter, usually right
across the street from the famous Café du Monde. Often
we would set up a microphone, play some records to try
to draw a crowd, sing, and finally the designate for the
evening would preach. Often there was no overt response
at all. Few, if any, would show any interest in what we
were doing. So many crazy things were happening right
in that area that the people who were regular occupants
of that section of the city just became oblivious to most of
the things going on. But I remember that when we made
that trek back on the bus to our seminary campus and
evaluated the results of our evening's efforts, someone
would always say, "Well, we did our job. God's Word will
not return to Him void."

So we can do a better job. Everyone agrees with that.
The question is, "How?" Who's got the key? Well, there
are several things that would help us put our hands on
that key and begin to use it effectively.

Have you ever been driving down the street in your
car, maybe listening to the news on the radio, when sud-

denly you realize that your wife or one of your children has been talking to you for some time and you haven't even heard a word? I have to confess that's happened to me. When our children were young, that would happen occasionally. I would be driving someplace with them in the car. My mind would be a thousand miles away and they would say, "Daddy! Daddy! DADDY!" When I finally gave them my attention, they would always ask, "Daddy, why weren't you listening to me?"

That's a good question. Why don't we listen? Why is it that so often someone is speaking to us and we just mentally turn him off? Dick Innes says that God has given us a filter system for our minds that serves as a defense mechanism.[4] It keeps us from being overwhelmed with all the incoming messages that are directed our way. Do you realize that there are thousands of stimuli directed toward us each day? There is so much, in fact, that our minds are not capable of sorting out all of them and making sense of what we hear or see. So the mind just blocks off what it doesn't want to take in.

Just think of the incoming messages directed at you . . . newspapers, TV, billboards, posters, bumper stickers, mail, radio advertisements, announcements at church . . . on and on. We can't handle all that effectively, so we sort out what we want and what we don't.

> On the average, this is what happens: Out of every one hundred people who are actually exposed to a television commercial, thirty actually attend to its content; that is they know what is being said; fifteen understand the content (one-half of those who attend to it initially); and only five retain its content in active memory twenty-four hours later.
>
> This is a graphic illustration of how the human perceptual filter selectively screens incoming information. These kinds of effects are not confined to the commercial world. There are thousands of published

and unpublished studies documenting selective screening in all phases of life.[5]

Those of us who have a message to communicate must understand that simply throwing it out in hopes that someone will hear is not the answer. The fact that we give a message by no means indicates that we have indeed communicated that message.

Give Me Another Handle

Other considerations will help us find the key to sharing the message God has given us. Realize that information is processed. Specialists in sales who are constantly studying how and why people hear their messages tell us that all of us exercise what is known as "selective exposure, selective attention, selective comprehension, selective perception, selective distortion, and selective retention."[6]

Understanding these categories would help us get another handle on our task.

Selective Exposure. Simply said, this means you and I listen to what we want to hear. People want their biases, their convictions, their prejudices reinforced. So we are attuned to others who voice those things we have already decided about, and we listen to messages that reaffirm our thinking. Innes says:

> Because people see and hear only what they want to see and hear, they tend to expose themselves only to messages that strengthen their present beliefs and attitudes, and avoid any message they perceive to be irrelevant to their needs or threatening to their personal views, opinions, or convictions.[7]

This presents, of course, a tremendous challenge to those who are trying to share the Christian gospel.

Selective Attention. This is the process whereby each of us decides whether or not we will respond to what we hear. My teenage boys are prime examples. They hear me amazingly well when I call to them, "Hey gang, I'm going to the ball game. Anybody want to go?" They get that message loud and clear. On the other hand, I can say very distinctly, "I'd like for you guys to help me mow the lawn this morning." No one seems to hear that. If I question why no one responded, the reply is often, "Oh, I didn't hear you say that, Dad." You see, everyone gives attention to what he chooses to hear.

Selective Comprehension. Once again the stimuli directed toward our brain can be accepted as being pertinent to us, but that acceptance does not guarantee that we will comprehend fully or that the message will be accurately perceived. Not long ago our sons and I were watching baseball's major league all-star game. The boys were rooting for the National League. I was pulling for the American League team. There was a close play at first base in which the American League runner was called safe. My sons began a loud, long cry that the umpire had missed the call. Apparently it was close enough that the announcers figured they would show it again in slow motion on the instant replay. This time it was certain. The announcers pointed out how the runner had beaten the throw by half a step. I cheered to know that I had seen the play correctly. But those boys wouldn't give up. The announcers were crazy! The ump was blind! Somehow they had seen something different. Do you see what I'm saying? We are selective in what we comprehend or perceive accurately. Our perception depends on many other factors, including our own biases.

Selective Distortion. People not only see what they want to see; they distort the message to say what they want it to say. Innes says that a person with low self-esteem will take a genuine compliment and make it an attempt at manipulation. Since that person thinks so poorly of himself, he cannot imagine someone really paying him a compliment. In his perception, he imagines that the person is somehow trying to take advantage of him. So he takes a positive communication and makes it negative.

Selective Retention. The things we remember are highly selective. Our minds are unbelievable creations. They are capable of storing an estimated 100 trillion bits of information. Compared to a computer which only has the capacity for billions, the human mind has no equal. But that mind often forgets. In the September 29, 1986 issue of *Newsweek* magazine, cognitive psychologist Ulric Neisser of Emory University said that people remember certain things because they rehearse those things that interest them. For instance, a well-known fact is that people in a certain age group know exactly where they were and what they were doing when they received the news that President John F. Kennedy had been shot. Neisser says that their vivid recall of November 22, 1963, is the product of a simple emotion. "You think about these special events a lot," he says. All kinds of "events" come to most people's minds without any problem. That "first kiss" is never forgotten. The memories of the first day at school or the first car that one owned are locked away forever. The explanation is the rehearsing of these experiences that is done all the way through life. We choose to remember.

Thomas Crook of the Memory Assessment Clinic says in the same *Newsweek* article that the more we relive a memory, the more permanent it becomes—even if the accuracy is distorted. Professor Cameron Camp of the University of New Orleans suggests that memory defects of older people may be as simple as a decision, not necessarily conscious, to sweep out the mind. Older people are less likely to encounter really memorable information and more willing to forget what they learn because they judge it unworthy to remember. Scientists increasingly concur that we are extremely selective, increasingly selective in what we remember.

As a pastor, I am always interested in the things that people really hear and the things they remember from my messages. Often it is that funny illustration or that sad story that was used to illustrate a point. Interestingly enough, they do not remember the point of the story nearly as well as the illustration.

Once again, our memory is directly related to our prejudices, our biases, our convictions, our beliefs. We are much more willing to allow something to stick in our memory if it confirms our values, touches our emotions, validates those things on which we place importance. Myers and Reynolds write:

> An idea, object, or event tends not even to enter the conscious mental stream unless it conforms reasonably well, not only with the things we have come to expect in our culture and society, but also with our personal interests, goals, and objectives of the moment. If it does not, it tends to be overlooked, ignored, forgotten immediately, or otherwise rejected; as far as our conscious mind is concerned, it simply doesn't exist.[8]

The key, then, to successfully sharing an idea is to speak to the need of the one who hears that message. There is no way to overemphasize that when it comes to speaking or showing the gospel to the person who does not know Christ. In our culture, from a human vantage point, it is impossible to share adequately the most important message at our disposal unless the one who hears the message is willing to listen. Most of the time that person will listen only if he or she senses that what is being shared meets a felt need in his or her life.

Hearers Have Needs

That brings us to a very important aspect of this whole issue of hearing the gospel. Apparently no human beings are completely satisfied with what and who they are. No society or culture seems to provide all the answers to the questions of life. The problems which are uncared for or inadequately dealt with by one's cultural system are commonly referred to as "felt needs." These are needs that may be felt on a surface level or at a much deeper level. Surface-level needs are the obvious such as food, shelter, money, health. They are easy to see and articulate. Deeper needs such as a desire to love and be loved and the need to have purpose in life are not so easy to identify and talk about. The perceptive and effective communicator is the person who is able to read these needs, particularly the surface needs, and adapt his message to address them.

When Jesus related to people, such as the rich young man (Matt. 19:16-22) and the blind Bartimaeus (Mark 10:46-52), they told him of a need. He dealt with that before he moved on to a deeper need in their life. The same was true in the Lord's relationship with his disciples. Often their needs were couched in questions that they asked their Master. Each time He dealt with that need, often using it as a point of reference to deal with other, deeper needs.

Realize that the communicator is dealing with perception. And to the person with needs, the perception is just as important as the reality. The perceived or felt need in a person's life must be addressed before that person will allow one to deal with the deeper need that is there. The communicator must scratch where there is an itch before the listener will allow further digging into the less obvious aspects of his life.

Every pastor has repeated illustrations of this truth. A disturbed young man came to my office late one winter evening. Face flushed, eyes heavy with grief yet darting quickly from place to place as he talked, he began to pour out his hurt. He told a story far too familiar. His wife had left him. The reasons were multiple: preoccupation with success, money, a career that took center stage. She had been lonely, left with young children and little adult companionship, rootless in another new city that her husband's work demanded. Now she was gone. His hurt was overwhelming. As we talked, however, the conversation shifted a bit. From the preeminence of his hurt there began to surface the whole issue of guilt, wrong priorities, failure to live up to marital commitments.

Soon the young man's relationship with the church and then with God began to surface. He confessed that he needed someone beyond himself, someone with greater strength that could help him see his way out of the crisis of his life. At that point I could deal with his real need—a new life, a personal relationship with Jesus Christ, forgiveness of his sin—rather than simply the felt needs that had brought him to my office.

That illustration, by the way, had a beautiful ending. The young man accepted Jesus Christ into his life. He began immediately to act out his new faith in the context of the church. In a few months his estranged wife saw something different in his life, was attracted to what she saw and at the same time disillusioned with the romance that once seemed to offer a solution to her needs. Soon that wife returned to her husband. He willingly accepted her home and introduced her to the Savior who had made all the difference in his life.

If the message of Christ is to be communicated adequately, the process usually involves (a) the identification of a felt need and the agreement by both interactants that it is indeed a felt need, (b) dealing with the felt need, and in the process (c) identifying and raising to the level of felt needs one or more deeper needs, (d) dealing with one or more of these, and (e) discovering and then dealing with one or more others as the process continues.[9]

Felt needs are the key to opening a person's heart and mind so Christ's message can penetrate the defenses that have been set up to prohibit the messages one does not want. When a listener hears the messages that seem to solve his problems, he is all ears. His ears are open to hear; his eyes are open to see.

A number of years ago a wonderful lady in the congregation I served in Nashville, Tennessee, was stricken with a terrible, life-destroying cancer. She was confined to her bed at home for a long time and finally she became a long-time resident at Vanderbilt Hospital. I'll never forget visiting with her one day when she said, "Don, you know what I want to hear? I don't care a thing in the world about the statistics that tell me how many patients who have my disease die with it. I'm not interested in the doctor's describing for me all the intricacies of this terrible illness and how they intend to treat it. I don't want someone to lament what a terrible situation this is. All I want to hear is that they have found a cure. I want someone to walk in that door and say, 'Ruth, we've discovered a cure! You are going to get well!' That's all I'm interested in right now."

Our world is interested in hearing that a cure has been discovered . . . for their hurt, their grief, their guilt, their shame, their fear, their worry. When I am afraid, I want someone to help me not be afraid. When I am lonely, I want someone or something to help eliminate that loneliness. Those are "felt needs," and when someone speaks to those, my mind and heart are open to hearing his message.

Here Jesus ministered. He dealt with the whole person, caring and loving, healing and helping. Often when He had dealt with that surface need, He then pointed persons to a much less obvious but more important need in their lives. He said to the woman brought to him in adultery:

" 'Woman, where are they? Has no one condemned you?' 'No one, sir,' she said. 'Then neither do I condemn

you,' Jesus declared. 'Go now and leave your life of sin' "
(John 8:10*b*-11).

He dealt not only with the immediate, felt need. He
dealt with the real problem in her life, the problem of sin.
"Go now and leave your life of sin."

Opening that Lock

Dick Innes clarifies for us the method the communicator uses to insert the key and open the lock to the minds
of unbelievers.[10] The mental filter is a God-given device
for our own protection. No matter how hard we try, it is
impossible to screen out all the stimuli that come our way.
God understood that this filter system could be used to
filter out His message as well as those that were destruc-
tive to the individual. So he provided a way. He built into
us the willingness to open that mind and heart when
the felt need was dealt with. The most effective way of
communicating with an audience or an individual is to
determine what that particular group or that individual
feel they need and to target that need for your remarks.
That will open every locked mind so the gospel can be
presented.

Notes

1. James F. Engel and H. Wilbert Norton, *What's Gone Wrong with
the Harvest? A Communication Strategy for the Church and World
Evangelism* (Grand Rapids: Zondervan Publishing House, 1975), p. 34.

2. Ibid., p. 35. The outline is the outline used in this book.

3. Dick Innes, *I Hate Witnessing* (Ventura, California: Regal Books,
1985), p. 146.

4. Ibid., p. 142.

5. Ibid., p. 143.

6. Ibid., p. 148.

7. Ibid.

8. James H. Myers and William H. Reynolds, *Consumer Behavior and Marketing Management* (Boston: Houghton, Mifflin Company, 1967), p. 134.

9. Charles H. Kraft, *Communication Theory for Christian Witness* (Nashville: Abingdon Press, 1983), p. 92.

10. Innes, p. 152.

7

A Cure for Stopped-Up Ears

When I was a boy, the swimming pools were always filled with people in the summer. The kids swimming were trying to avoid that 100°-plus Texas weather, and swimming was a good way to do it.

I always admired the divers with their long, slender builds, their bleached blonde hair, and that marvelous ability to do a backward somersault or a beautiful gainer off the high board. Somehow, everytime I saw them do that, I believed that I could do it too. And I still believe I could have . . . if it hadn't been for my ears and nose.

When the Lord built me, He didn't intend for me to be a diver. No one has ever been able to explain to me the exact reason, but my ears and my nostrils just can't stand being suddenly confronted by a lot of water. Every time I went into that pool head first I came out waterlogged. Half the pool went into my ears and nose. The next four hours were spent blowing my nose and shaking my head from side to side, trying to get the water out. Most of the time, the water finally leaked out of my ears onto my pillow as I slept. At any rate, diving just wasn't worth it.

I tried everything. Do you remember the nose guards that pinched your nose and made you sound like you had a terrible cold? I tried those. They never really worked. Nor did the earplugs. Somehow they refused to keep the water out completely. They were too loose to do that. But they did keep you from hearing.

I remember going swimming with a buddy one day and seeing all that beautiful diving. The same old urge revived in me, and I decided on the spot that I was going to dive that day. There was a swim shop at the pool where you could buy earplugs. So I went in and bought a pair, stuffed them into my ears, and headed for the low diving board. (When you rarely dive, it's better to start with the low board.)

Well, a couple of hours went by. I had dived dozens of times, was completely worn out, and had two ears and a nose full of water. I finally decided to call it quits and looked around for my buddy to tell him I was ready to head for home. He was nowhere to be found. I asked around, and several people said that his mother had picked him up an hour ago and he was gone. You talk about disgusted! I was fit to be tied. (That's an old Texas expression for "furious.") He had left me there alone without a ride!

As soon as I got home, about an hour later, I called the guy I now considered my ex-friend. I wanted to tell him how much fun it was to walk home with no shoes since the pavement was hot enough to fry an egg on it. When I began my tirade about his inconsiderate attitude, he stopped me in my tracks. "Don," he said, "wait just one minute. Don't blame me for this. I tried. I yelled and yelled at you to tell you we were leaving. You never even acted like you heard me. You just kept on diving. I figured you just wanted to stay. I was ready to go. So I left!"

Later it dawned on me that my friend had told it exactly like it was. He had tried to get my attention and couldn't. You see, my ears were shut. I couldn't hear. Water, yes! Words, no! He had tried to give me the message that I needed, but my ears were clogged with plugs and water. So I went on doing something that I thought was great fun at the moment. But it was very costly to my feet just about an hour later.

Check Their Plugs

For several chapters now we've been talking about the need to share Christ with that lost world that Jesus saw. Our Lord wept over the lostness of our world and left His people with the divine imperative to share the message of His death, burial, resurrection, ascension, and coming again. And we want to be obedient to that command. Our problem is that sometimes we try, but the world can't hear.

Our difficulty is similar to the one my friend faced. He "yelled and yelled" but I paid no attention. You see, I had two problems. I was preoccupied with what I was doing and my ears were stopped up. If only someone could have gotten my attention and taken the plugs out of my ears, I would have gladly heard the message.

That story is analogous to what is happening spiritually to men and women all around us. They have plugs in their ears. Sometimes we shout and shout the message they need, but they can't hear.

When we try to witness to the lost persons of the latter part of the twentieth century, it would be wise to check their plugs. There are multiple causes that keep them from hearing. Consider the following:

The Rise of Secularism

Our culture is increasingly becoming a secular society. The *Oxford English Dictionary* defines secular as "belonging to the world and its affairs, as distinguished from the church and religion, not concerned with or devoted to religion, caring for the present only."

Secularism is spelled out as being "the doctrine that morality should be based solely in regard to the well-being of mankind in the present life, to the exclusion of all considerations drawn from belief in God or in a future state."

That is an accurate description of the culture most of us live in. There's a widespread tendency to live for today and exclude all considerations of God or His desires for our lives. This is nothing new, of course, since the seeds of secularism have been germinating since Adam pronounced his independence from God. Genesis' opening chapters describe the results of that kind of thinking. Adam and his offspring began to reap the results of a self-declared independence from God. By the time we read chapter 11 of Genesis, we see rebellion in full bloom. "And they said, Go to, let us build us a city and a tower, whose top may reach into heaven; and let us make us a name, lest we be scattered abroad upon the face of the whole earth" (Gen. 11:4, KJV). This tower is the first monument recorded in Scripture to man's attempt to be independent of God.

Secularism is a pervading influence in our world today. Its rise has been evident in the northern and western parts of the United States for many years. Only recently, however, has it made substantial inroads into the areas once known as the "Bible belt" of our country. Charlotte, North Carolina became the first southern city to require zoning permits for churches in 1984. In the fall of '84 the city council of that southern city passed a law that required churches in residential areas to get a special use permit in order to receive zoning permits so that a church building could be built. Added to that were stringent building codes, landscaping codes, and a ceiling that said no building of worship that exceeded 1199 people could be built in a residential area of the city without permission of the city council.

To meet these requirements, churches must spend multiplied thousands of dollars and are still severely limited in growth. The attitude of many on the city council and the community at large seemed to be that there was little sympathy with the mission of the church to reach the city for Jesus Christ. Harvey Cox in his book *The Secular City* said, "It is not the intention of secular man to destroy the church, but simply to render it innocuous."[1]

The plight of churches in Charlotte has become the pattern for other cities throughout our nation. As our nation and our cities become more and more secular, it is more difficult for the cause of Christ to be heard. In southern cities such as Atlanta, Dallas, and Raleigh, the struggle between the values of secular man and the church have already surfaced. The future will produce more of those kinds of problems.

The rise of secularism is one of the plugs in the ears of modern man.

Mastery and Self-Sufficiency

When that first man sinned against God and declared his independence, he began to relate all matters of truth and morality to himself. He declared that he would decide right and wrong, good and bad. He would assume the focal point of deciding truth and error. But God did not create man with this in mind. The end result is tragedy and chaos. Man assumes that he is "master of his fate" and sufficient in himself to deal with life's issues, and God allows it all to happen. But God also allows the consequences of such decisions to come about. In our day of increasing secularism, we see marriages crumble, children who rebel, lives destroyed by alcohol and drugs, courts void of real justice, political leaders with no integrity. All of this serves as plugs in the ears of those who are stumbling in the dark and cannot hear the voice of the Redeemer.

Amusement and Diversion

Who would debate that we are bombarded with sounds and sights that are designed to keep us from any serious thinking? Few of us sit down and contemplate the mysteries of life. Our hurry-up, get-it-done society has very little patience with the person who would like to contemplate what life is all about.

Think of the enormous number of opportunities we have to be amused. The original meaning of the word *muse* was "to think." To be a-mused is to "not think." So the more we are amused, the more we keep from thinking. Many people in the area of the country where I live watch a TV show called "Entertainment Tonight" each evening. Sometimes, when I am home, my wife and I watch it since it follows the evening news. I am always amazed at the fact that a TV program can fill each evening, five days a week, with news about the people who amuse us. That in itself shows how much there is all about us to keep us from thinking too seriously. Video games, movies, sports events, TV—the list is endless. All of this has the same effect . . . it keeps us from dealing with the more serious issues of life and death.

The lost person prefers a busy mind. He is then not reminded of the separation he intuitively feels inside. But you can be certain that diversions are a very formidable plug in the ear of the unbeliever. It's hard for the "still, small voice of God" to get your attention when your attention is turned to the blare of rock music or the roar of the crowd.

Busy Routines

Isn't it interesting, in the day of unbelievable technology that should abbreviate our work experience, that people are so busy. We are, in fact, so busy that to get quiet and alone with God is difficult. Even Christians complain that they can't find time for a few minutes to read their Bibles and be alone with the Father. Unbelievers are so busy with crammed schedules and hectic demands that they can't even imagine a life-style that would advocate solitude and reflection. A commencement speaker at a college graduation revealed the results of an interesting study of a group of adults, all over ninety-five years old. They were asked one question: "If you had life to do over again, what would you do differently?" Three responses rang loud and clear. They were:

Reflect More. The senior adults said that they would stop and think more about who you are, what you have, and what you want to become. That's good advice but it's rarely adhered to in our day. Could it be that God provided the Lord's day for that very thing? People rarely see that anymore. If you don't believe that, go to the shopping center on Sunday in any major city and see the people of this era insisting that we make the first day of the week just another working day. Little reflection occurs when there is a constant push.

Take More Risk. Those who had lived ninety-plus years insisted that life is made up of risk. Not the immature, foolish kind of risk. But risking who you are and what you have on things that have eternal qualities. To do that, you must have a goal and purpose in life. Before goals and purposes can be established, much questioning must occur. What makes life worth living? What is life really about? What does God want of me? How many people do you know asking or even thinking about those kinds of questions? Most of us are too busy.

Do More Things that Will Last Forever. Finally, that group said they would try to do something with the time that they had been given that would outlast their stay. I suppose that the closer a person comes to leaving, the more that has meaning. Unfortunately, our culture is so busy that this kind of thinking is postponed for the golden years. Too bad that many of us will never make it that far, so the thinking, the contemplating, the musing will never take place.

Busy routines are one of the plugs that fill the ears and mute the voice of God.

Pulling the Plugs

God wants our attention! To get it he uses many different techniques. Most of them involve media. Unlike my friend who screamed at me when he was preparing to leave the swimming pool but, failing to get appropriate response, left me there, God uses many ways to transmit the message He wants us to hear. The Bible is filled with examples of that truth. Media . . . God both shows and tells. He speaks His message and then dramatizes it so that every type of person may be able to comprehend it. In turn, God's word for us is, "Pull the plugs!" Explore the possibilities. Check out the alternatives. Realize that loud proclamation may reach some, but others need different methods. Our task is to get those plugs out of the listeners' ears so they can discover the message God has for them.

Do you understand there are some people who would be absolutely bored to death with a magnificent message that was preached by the most eloquent of preachers? But that same person would gladly respond to the warmth and caring of a small group who act out the gospel of love. One person prefers the intellectual challenge of reading a good book by C. S. Lewis or Sheldon Van Aucoin, while another would gravitate to the movies that deal with challenges of rearing children like those presented by James Dobson and Kevin Lehman. Perhaps the mediagraphy provided in this book will be helpful and will suggest the wide range of resources available.

Hear me when I say, *"The same medicine doesn't work on all people."* But our Lord has designed our uniqueness and our needs so that there are ways everyone can be reached.

A mistake is made, I believe, when you and I insist that everyone must conform to our interests and our taste. God made a diverse world. Certainly our secular world recognizes that. Think of the multiplicity of interests that are appealed to by the secular media. TV alone has almost every interest that one might have shown weekly to grab the attention of the viewing audience. Game shows, dramas, sporting events, sit coms, Shakespeare, "how to" programs, news, special events—on and on. Why so many? Why such a variation of programming? Because people think differently, see life differently, have different values, have a different understanding of life, find different things appealing. As believers and church leaders, our tendency is often to provide one diet and insist that everyone eat and enjoy it.

We are currently experiencing a time that some are calling the "era of the Super Church." Like no other time in recent history, the Southern Baptists and other groups as well are experiencing the rise of very large congregations. Many suggestions have been made to explain the phenomena. Certainly there is no one reason that can be pointed to as the single reason for this kind of growth pattern. One possibility is quite important for us to consider.

Churches can be compared to supermarkets and the neighborhood grocery store. There was a day when everyone shopped at their neighborhood grocery. They were known there. That's where their friends shopped. They felt comfortable and secure, that their store offered as fine a shopping opportunity as they might want. It was part of their culture . . . the way things were done. Today all that has changed. The era of the neighborhood grocery has gone. When people shop, they seek out supermarkets. They are looking for diversity in shopping opportunities. The amenities, the extras, unusual things that can only be offered in a larger store now appeal to the majority of people. They want a "one-stop shopping" experience. They want plenty of parking space, and they even enjoy a certain amount of anonymity.

Churches have followed much the same pattern. Particularly in urban settings, people seek out the church which offers multiple opportunities. They want programs . . . choirs, programs for their teenagers and children, ministries to the aging, social ministries, drama groups, multiple staffs that oversee a complex ministry. Why has this become part of our expectations? Diversity! People are not the same. They have different needs and desires, and they want those needs provided for.

All of this relates directly to media. Few instruments offer such a clear-cut opportunity to "unplug the ears" of those who cannot and will not hear as does media. Media is music . . . soft, loud, sophisticated, casual, country, and the symphony. Music speaks to many people in ways a sermon never would. A good example was the climax of a multi-million-dollar event that took place in the summer of 1986. America was celebrating the refurbishing of "the Lady," the Statue of Liberty. For an entire weekend, the rich and the famous made television appearances to laud America's good fortune to have such a symbol. The final night was a giant celebration that was nationally televised from the Meadow Grounds in New Jersey. The evening had been spectacular. It featured every well-known secular artist from Willie Nelson to Patti La Belle. But for the final few moments there were beautiful scenes of our country flashed on the screen, while in the background the most beautiful rendition of the national anthem imaginable was sung. Little reference was made to the person singing the "Star-Spangled Banner." The next evening, however, the anchor for ABC News said that calls had come in all day from all over the country asking the identity of the woman who sang the national anthem. He announced that her name was Sandi Patti. She was a Christian music artist and her records and tapes were well known among the Christian community.

In our town, the phones rang off the wall of our local disk jockeys too. I heard one program where caller after caller tried to identify the singer who electrified America with her voice. When the DJs said that her music could be purchased from Christian book stores, the response was always, "Well, I'm on my way! I want to hear more of that kind of singing."

Imagine, will you, the enormous impact for Christ that one event could, and perhaps did, have on those who would never darken the door of a church to hear a message preached. That one experience had the potential of removing thousands, millions of plugs that had kept people from hearing.

The potential of media is unlimited! After all, every time we communicate, we do it with media. Music, books, tapes, pictures, movies, TV, radio, newspapers, tracts, sermons, sign, testimonies, billboards, people—all are media. If we communicate at all, we do it through some form of media. But not every person can be reached with the same instrument. Our task, then, is to be wise and sensitive to as many people as possible. We want to fulfill the Great Commission and go to all the world . . . culturally, educationally, vocationally, socially, geographically. And the way we do that is through media.

Never before have the resources been available that are currently accessible. Rarely have Christians had the opportunity to so impact this world as we do today. So we want to explore every avenue to see how best we unplug those ears.

Note

1. Harvey Cox, *Secular City* (New York: Macmillan, 1966).

8
Keeping On Keeping On

Julia Woodward served as a missionary in Ecuador for fifty years. While there she worked with a very primitive tribe of Indians. During those years she reduced the people's language into written form, taught them to read and write, and began to translate the Scripture into their language. But though she accomplished all this in her fifty years on the mission field, fewer than a handful of people came to know Christ.[1]

Something interesting happened, however, when Miss Woodward retired. A missionary couple, the Henry Clawsons, followed her as missionaries to that same tribe and the results they experienced were phenomenal. Almost an entire tribe of 15,000 came to know Christ within the next fifteen years.

A principle of evangelism can be learned from that story. Dick Innes said:

> People who have never heard the Gospel, or those who have a low level of understanding the Gospel, as a general rule do not come to Christ without preparation of mind and heart. For most, depending on their background and experience, raising their level of God-consciousness and Gospel awareness is a process which takes place over a period of time.[2]

The Clawsons were able to communicate the good news because of the faithful sowing of Miss Woodward.

Earlier we dealt with another principle that bears repeating. Innes points to the principle of selective exposure as equally important to everyone interested in media.

> Because people see and hear only what they want to see and hear, they tend to expose themselves only to messages that strengthen their present beliefs and attitudes, and avoid any message they perceive to be irrelevant to their needs or threatening to their personal views, opinions, or convictions.[3]

The two principles mentioned here are solid indicators that some advance work needs to be done in the life of the unbeliever before there is any real chance of impacting his life through church attendance and Bible study. Most people who do not have a religious background with a Christian orientation care little about church and Sunday School and the other things that seem important to Christians. Nothing is more of a "turn-off" than for some well-meaning friend or neighbor to keep on inviting an unchurched, uninterested person to church. Try to imagine your friend from India who constantly badgers you about attending his Hindu temple with him. He offers to pick you up, take your children, whatever it takes to get you there. But you don't want to go. You have no interest whatsoever. You imagine how awful, how unfamiliar, how awkward you would feel just being there. Often those are the exact feelings of the people we are trying to evangelize.

Then how do we begin to overcome the barriers and open the door for dialogue and sharing? Some of the ways are familiar to us. They have been used many times, even though they may not have found their way into a book as a method of evangelism. Let me suggest a few of the "old" ways:

Give Them a Book

For several years I served in both the army chaplaincy and in the local church as a counselor. People came to me with problems that at times seemed almost beyond belief. During those years I discovered that one of the best ways to sow seeds, establish some thinking patterns, and address both felt and real needs in an individual's life was through books.

Recently I was sitting in the barber's chair getting a haircut. There were men in several of the chairs, both in front of me and to my side, who were discussing various issues that involved their personal lives. I always enjoy the role of pastor when I am incognito. The guys think I am one of them so they just open up and "let it all hang out." That was happening that day in the barber shop. They were talking about their women, their problems, their fears. It reminded me of dozens of other occasions where someone opened their life and I was able to say, "Have you read Chuck Swindoll's book *You and Your Child?*" or "A guy named James Dobson has a book that I've been reading on that very problem. He really says some important things that might be helpful to you. I'll loan the book to you."

I believe that one of the most powerful forces we have as Christians to stimulate thinking and establish a base of discussion is through books that deal with "felt needs" but also present the good news. People everywhere are looking for answers. We live in the information revolution. People will read if they feel what they read addresses their issue. This is particularly true when living is difficult and answers don't come easily.

Robert Ornstein in his book *Multimind* says that we are extremely sensitive to

> recent information, emotional upsets like bad feelings last for a while, then are forgiven. Terrible disasters

like an air crash force attention on airliners for a while; all sorts of reforms are initiated and then the spotlight goes away. We are interested only in "the news," the sudden appearance of something unknown. Unexpected or extraordinary events seem to have fast access to consciousness, while an unchanging background noise, a constant weight, or a chronic problem soon gets shunted into the background. It is easy to raise money for emergencies, like the few victims of a well-publicized disaster: it is much more difficult to raise money for the many victims of continuous malnutrition . . . gradual changes in the world go unnoted while sharp changes are immediately seized on by the mind.[4]

Ornstein further points out that when a personal crisis has arisen, the heart and mind are often open to your message as during few other times. Give them a book with the message of hope in its content. Give them a book that speaks to their hurt, scratches where they itch. Then make sure that they know how this particular need and other issues in their life can be addressed.

Let me suggest a few occasions when books can be useful.

1. Where There Is a Death or Dying

Books continue to flood the shelves of book stores and libraries that speak to the issue of death and dying. More good material is available now than ever before. Far too many church leaders are relatively unfamiliar with the tremendous impact that a good book can have in the lives of those who are walking through the valley of the shadow of death. Let me suggest some of those books that may stimulate the reader to do some further looking for books in this category that might be valuable tools in evangelism.

A. *Good Grief* by Granger Westberg. Fortress Press,

1962. This significant little book was written by a Lutheran minister/counselor after a study of the famous Coconut Grove fire in Los Angeles, California, in 1948. It was the first serious study of its kind done on grief. *Good Grief* traces the stages of grief and often helps persons experiencing grief to understand that what they are feeling is natural. While the book doesn't deal specifically with the gospel, it sows seeds that can be tremendously helpful and beneficial for sharing the gospel with one who is grieving.

B. *Mourning Song* by Joyce Landorf. Fleming H. Revell, 1974. A lady whom I had never seen came into my office one day. She had heard that our church provided counseling, and she was desperate for help. After we talked for a few moments, I found that she had a mother who was dying in another state and she herself was grieving so badly that she felt that she too was going to die.

That morning I did not talk long with my visitor. Instead I suggested to her that I wanted to pray for her. After that prayer time I placed in her hands a copy of *Mourning Song*. My advice was to read Landorf's poignant description of her own feelings during the time of her mother's dying and death. "When you've completed the book," I said, "come back to see me. I want to talk with you again."

About two weeks later that lady came back to my office. She had read the book. Some parts she had read repeatedly. We talked about grief, parents, mortality, our own death. Though she had no church background of any kind and no sense of need for the church, her life at that moment was wide open for the sharing of the gospel. I told her of a God who not only would walk with her during this crisis, but who would be her Savior, her Redeemer, her Lord when she too stood at the moment of death. In the weeks that followed, she opened her life to Jesus Christ.

C. *Other Books on Grief.* There are many other excel-

lent books that deal with the subject of grief. Joseph Bayly
has written an excellent book, *The Last Thing We Talk
About* (Scripture Union, 1979), that speaks to the need of
hurting parents who have lost children. C. S. Lewis and
Sheldon Van Aucoin have both written books dealing
with personal loss. Martin Marty's *A Cry of Absence*
(Harper, 1983) guides the reader through an inner quest
for the true meaning of crisis, when bleakness grips the
soul and even God seems absent. Warren Wiersbe in his
book *Why Us?* (Fleming H. Revell, 1983) tackles the most
difficult questions that men and women face: personal
suffering, why do bad things happen to good people, what
is the purpose of life, is there a God, the problem of evil.
His approach is simple, warm, empathetic.

Few books in this category are more perceptive and
encouraging than Ron Lee Davis' book *Gold in the Making* (Thomas Nelson, 1984). It was written following the
sudden death of his father. His mother was diagnosed as
having a tumor, and his daughter, born eleven weeks
premature, contracted numerous lung infections and
lived in isolation for over a year. Davis' book speaks to
believer and nonbeliever alike about the problems of
grief, pain, and suffering.

I could go on and on, but the point is that no one need
walk through the valleys of life alone. Many writers can
introduce us to methods of coping. More importantly,
those writers can become the instruments that God can
use to introduce others to the one who has promised his
grief-stricken disciples, "I will pray the Father, and He
will give you another Counselor, to be with you for ever
. . . I will not leave you desolate; I will come to you" (John
14:16,18, RSV).

2. Where There Is Separation or Divorce

Last summer my wife asked me to go to the grocery to
pick up some things while she went to the beauty shop for

her weekly delight. It's interesting to me that people pick unusual places these days to get a little counseling. Marriage problems seemed to be the order of the day. No sooner had I chosen my cart, picked up a few strawberries and a banana or two, than it all began. As I pulled up to the scales where the produce is weighed, I overheard two ladies in front of me talking about their separations. It was a kind of one-upsmanship situation as one tried to describe the difficulties that her "ex" was causing her. I could sense a real animosity against men in general developing, so I quickly pushed my shopping cart on down the aisle.

Then somewhere around the cereal aisle a person I hardly knew stopped me and wanted some "on the spot" advice. It seems that a friend's husband was involved with another woman; the family was torn apart. The friend was having to make a decision about whether to move out or not, and the lady who had pulled me over wanted to know what I would advise.

When I got home I started putting up the groceries, my wife came in from the beauty shop. She had just had a long conversation with her beauty operator about the problems with her children that were caused by the divorce she was walking through. By this time I had a clear and distinct message: Our world is hurting in the area of marriage and family. And people don't know where to turn.

Actually, that message had come home to me long before my day at the grocery store. Everywhere I turn people are asking for help with their marriages, separations, divorces. Interestingly enough, many of the people who are open to a word from me . . . and from you . . . are people who never darken the door of anybody's church. They gave it their best shot and they have failed miserably. Now they are willing to listen to anybody who can help.

That's where books come in handy. So many times when you and I have reservations about voicing our advice, we can say it through a book.

Often a marriage is caught up in a whirlwind of problems that can be improved and even corrected with a minimum of help. The partner may need encouragement, a challenge to "hang in there." He or she is looking for some help to modify the patterns that are contributing to their problems. A sensitive Christian friend is an enormous asset when he can put into the hands of hurting people books like Gary Chapman's *Hope for the Separated: Wounded Marriages Can Be Healed* (Moody, 1982) or David Augsburger's *Caring Enough to Confront* (Regal, 1973). Jim Conway and his wife, Sally, have dealt with the time in life when many marriage problems occur— mid-life. He wrote *Men in Mid-Life Crisis* (David C. Cook, 1978). She later produced a book entitled *You and Your Husband's Mid-Life Crisis* (David C. Cook, 1982). Both give valuable insight to people who have been married for years but have hit some troubled waters.

Communication seems to always stand out as a primary problem in many marriages as well as families. No one addresses that better than Norman Wright. Two of his books are outstanding. *The Pillars of Marriage* (Regal, 1979) and *More Communication Keys for Your Marriage* (Regal, 1983) are valuable tools for a non-Christian friend who is struggling with a deteriorating marriage and wants help.

Some other excellent books that can provide encouragement are *Achieving the Impossible: Intimate Marriage* by Charles Sell (Ballantine, 1985); *The Joy of Committed Love* by Gary Smalley (Zondervan, 1984); *Saying Yes to Marriage* by William Willimon (Judson, 1979); *Magnificent Marriage* by Gordon MacDonald (Tyndale, 1976); *The Myth of the Greener Grass* by Allen

Petersen (Tyndale, 1983); and James Dobson's *Love Must Be Tough* (Word, 1983).

There are times, of course, when separation and divorce are already in progress. This is a time when people are unusually open, as they are in dying, to evaluating life and their needs for something or someone more substantial than they are currently experiencing. I find that there is no better time for persons to really hear than when they are walking through a divorce. Let me suggest a few books that can remove the "earplugs":

The Healing Divorce: a Practical and Theological Approach. This is available from Learnings Unlimited, 516 4th Ave., Congmont, CO 80501. The author has created a model of divorce recovery using the story of liberation of the children of Israel found in the biblical book of Exodus. He provides input on tapes and then accompanies them with a workbook entitled *The Healing Divorce Guidebook.*

Rebuilding: When Your Relationship Ends by Bruce Fisher (Impact, 1981). Fisher gives a description of the fifteen building blocks of divorce recovery that he located in his doctoral research. Books by Jim Smoke such as *Beyond Divorce: the Possibility of Remarriage* (Harvest House, 1985) and *Suddenly Single* (Fleming H. Revell, 1984) are very good. They are written with popular appeal but deal with substantive issues.

The books on the subject of divorce and remarriage fill the shelves of both secular and Christian book stores. Before recommending a book or an author, be sure that you have read the work and can know with a sense of assurance that this is the kind of book that will sensitize the reader to the gospel message. Be sensitive yourself to where the needy person is at that moment. Do your best to match the book with their "felt need."

3. When There Are Personal Needs

Everywhere I go, people are experiencing personal problems. These problems range from rebellious children to the loss of jobs. I've discovered that people with problems will read books. Let me give you some examples of the kind of books that appeal to hurting people. If children are the problem, give them books like Merton P. Strommen and A. Irene Strommen's *Five Cries of Parents* (Harper, 1985). Other good books which speak to this issue are Gary Smalley's *The Key to Your Child's Heart* (Word, 1984), David Elkind's *The Hurried Child* (Addison-Wesley, 1981), Guy Greenfield's *We Need Each Other* (Baker, 1984), and John M. Drescher's *Seven Things Children Need* (Herald, 1976). When job loss is the difficulty, place into their hands books like Richard Nelson Bolles' book, *What Color Is Your Parachute?* (Ten Speed, annual editions). Another book for this need is an older book by Richard Lathrop called *Who's Hiring Who?* (Ten Speed, 1977). Still another example is John L. Holland's *Making Vocational Choices* (Prentice-Hall, 1973).

These books can easily serve as tools to help a person get a handle on his problem. In addition, books can open doors to deal with more significant problems. The God-consciousness of a person has to be raised to the place where that person understands something of what the witness is saying. Books are key instruments in accomplishing that.

4. When a Personal Interest Is Discovered

Something as simple as an interest is often an open door. The media libraries of many churches are filled with books that deal with items of personal interest. If you have a friend interested in politics, give him a book from your media library such as *Ronald Reagan: In God I Trust.* It is a compilation of statements that President Reagan has made concerning his own relationship with God. Jimmy

Carter wrote *Why Not the Best?* (Broadman, 1977). Jack
and Jo Anne Hinckley described their ordeal when their
son shot President Reagan. This is an excellent book for
the political buff. Another book that might interest someone with this bent is Eugene B. McDaniel's book *Before
Honor* (Holman, 1975). It describes Navy Captain McDaniel's journey into the darkness of a communist prison.

Both men and women are often interested in sports
heroes. Encourage them to read Roger Staubach's *First
Down, Lifetime to Go* (Avon, 1976). UCLA's famous basketball coach, John Wooden, has written an excellent
book, *They Call Me Coach* (Word, 1984). Terry Bradshaw
of Pittsburgh Steeler fame wrote *Man of Steel* (Zondervan, 1979). Each of these may appeal to the person with
sports interest.

Other interests have equal appeal. There is the nature
lover who will be fascinated with all of James Herriot's
books. One newer book with special appeal is *James Herriot's Dog Stories* (St. Martin's, 1986). My favorite book in
this category is Peter Jenkins's *A Walk Across America*
(Morrow, 1979).

The best way to recommend a book to a friend is to
have read the book yourself. Then you can genuinely say,
"Have you read this book? I found it very interesting and
I knew you like this kind of thing. Maybe you'll enjoy it."
Ideally the book has a strong Christian testimony in it.
Many biographies are filled with statements concerning
the individual's commitment to Jesus Christ. Giving a
book with a powerful statement of faith is an excellent
way for adults and teenagers to share the reality of Christ
in their lives without seeming to be pushy or holier-than-
thou.

Don't stop with my suggestions. Imagine all the special
interest items that are in your church's media library.
Think about things that appeal to the women in your
community such as ceramics, quilting, golf, child care,

beauty tips, tennis, swimming, and so on. Who could you contact today? Who would read a book with a Christian message that God might use? When we begin to think in this way, the list becomes exhaustive.

5. Where There Are Children

Children love to read. One of the most successful things our media library does each summer is a children's Book Fair. Here boys and girls are challenged to take a trip with books. Many different approaches are used that will stimulate their imagination and get them started on reading. Most of the time there are more children in the media library than adults. They love to compete with each other for who can read the most books. And they just enjoy reading about their favorite characters or interests.

The shelves of our media library are filled with books that prick the interest of almost every child. Books such as *Brave Journey: Launching of the United States* by Mildred Corell Luckhardt and *Getting Along with Your Friends* (Abingdon, 1980) by Phyllis Reynolds Naylor appeal to older children. The younger boys and girls love books such as *The Stories Jesus Told* by Arthur W. Gross (Concordia, 1981). Books like the Dr. Seuss series have wide appeal to both age groups. Our shelves are stocked too with excellent reference books like *Webster's Color Dictionary, The First Encyclopedia,* and *Best Loved Selections from Children's Classics.* Obviously this list is endless. So many excellent books for children are being published. Your church media library worker is an excellent guide who can help you select appropriate books for the children with whom you wish to share.

The kind of ministry I'm describing can be very significant in all our churches. Many churches today have Mother's Morning Out programs or day schools or Latch Key Clubs. A majority of these children come from homes where there is little or no Christian influence. Often neither parent is a Christian. But that child is open to the good news, particularly when it is presented through the medium of books. Why not create a reading program for children in these special programs that involve both child and parent?

Expose the little ones to the gospel, but don't forget about their parents. While many of the adults would never come to church and would be resistant to a presentation of the gospel, they will read books. Be imaginative! In the summer, have a Book Club or Book Fair designed to reach the kids of the neighborhood. This has often been done with children in the church. Why not extend this great idea to involve those who need Christ so badly?

Take Them a Tape

Our world has become a world of tapes, both audio and video. Anyone can walk into a book store, a record shop, a radio or TV store, or now even convenience stores and have that statement confirmed. They are everywhere! Why? Because tapes are small, portable, convenient, and accessible. People in our society have become familiar with hearing the music or listening to the message they want simply by placing the audiotape in their car tape-player or in the stereo at home. Joggers run to the beat of music provided by tapes. Aerobics are done to the beat of music provided by tape. College lectures are taped. The antics of our children are recorded to be heard and viewed for a lifetime on tape. Tapes are a vital part of our entire cultural make-up.

That should give us a clue. To say that Christians need to maximize on the popularity of tapes is an understatement. Certainly the secular world has caught on. They are creating both audio- and videotapes for almost every interest and selling them as fast as they are produced. That means that many of us are buying them. In fact, the music and movie industry is exploding with the success of that little tape.

Certainly the Christian community wants to utilize this method of communication in the most productive way possible. Many churches see to it that their pastor's weekly messages are quickly reproduced on tape. This gives that traveling salesman a chance to hear the message over and over again as he travels during the week. It also provides an opportunity for him to share something meaningful that his pastor has said Sunday with a friend. Often God sees to it that a messenger speaks to just the problem or the need that a friend is dealing with. Tapes become an immediate resource that can be turned to for insight and help.

Evangelistic churches everywhere have become increasingly aware of the vital ministry that the distribution of tapes can have. One pastor shared that he received a phone call one day from a lady he'd never met who asked him to visit her home. When the pastor went the next day to that home, he was warmly greeted and ushered in to see the lady's husband, who was bedfast. As the pastor walked into the man's room, the invalid greeted him as if the two had known each other for years. They talked for a minute and the man began to thank the minister for the meaningful ministry that he had provided for him and his wife. "I don't understand," the pastor quizzed. "I've never met you or been in your home. How have I ministered to you?"

"Oh, I listen to you week after week. You see, our next-door neighbors go to your church. Each Sunday morning they stop by your media library and check out that week's tape. They bring it to us, and God uses it to touch our lives."

Now very interested, the pastor pursued the conversation, "Well, where do you go to church? Who is your pastor?"

The reply was direct, "Pastor, we've never gone to church. Our lives were too busy before I got sick. We never felt the need to go to church. But over this year that I've been confined to my bed and God has sent your ministry our way, I've opened up my heart and accepted Jesus Christ as my Savior. You are my pastor, really. I just wanted to meet you and know you personally."

I wonder how many times that story could be repeated. More importantly, I wonder how much God could really use this kind of ministry if our people could grasp the powerful tool that is at our fingertips.

Our church has followed the model of many other congregations in increasingly using and expanding our tape ministry. This past year my co-pastor, Bob Reccord, and I recorded an album of ten tapes with twenty messages called *Circling the Wagons: a Positive Word for Families in the Eighties.* This gave our people an opportunity to purchase the tapes and hear them again in their own families. It also provided an excellent Christmas gift, an anniversary present, a method of reaching out to friends who are walking through times when these sermons would touch a "felt need." It is surprising how many people will listen to a tape by a minister who would not feel comfortable at all in coming to hear him preach.

Many churches, obviously, have no means of producing tapes in their own local setting. They do not have the equipment and, therefore, cannot reproduce their pastor's messages. This in no way, however, prohibits a very effective tape ministry. Great numbers of tapes are being produced by various pastors and Christian speakers that can be purchased at a relatively inexpensive price. Some churches and tape clubs are now offering tapes for a love offering or no fee at all. Some tape ministries provide library services where one can simply check out the tape for two weeks. Then they pay only a small library fee and the price to mail the tape. Churches without a tape ministry should consider involving themselves in this kind of ministry so they can provide as many tapes as possible both to their congregation and to their community.

A new addition to the whole area of tape ministries is the rapid growth of videotapes. Baptists have not only entered into the arena of television broadcasting with the Baptist Telecommunication Network (BTN), ACTS, and others, but there is also a significant number of individual churches who will now provide videotape presentations of their various ministries. Add to that an increasing number of commercial manufacturers, and one can see the growing possibilities of ministry through videotapes.

For some time our church family has been using videotapes for training purposes. Numbers of companies are available who will provide quality materials for the training of leadership, teachers' meetings, and studies related to special interest groups. Now some materials are being produced that can be used evangelistically as well. A prime example of those kinds of materials is a video series produced in recent days by Evangelical Films called "Before You Say 'I Do'" and "After You Say 'I Do.'" These are video counseling series with workbooks designed to minister to people before they marry and shortly after they have taken that significant step. In these series subjects such as communication and conflict resolution, sexual intimacy and sexual dysfunction, and money management are addressed. Leading spokespersons in the areas such as H. Norman Wright, Tim and Beverly LaHaye, and Larry Burkett are featured. This kind of videotape is ideal to use in impacting people both in the church and outside with presentations that appeal to their "felt need."

There are numbers of ways that this material and others like it can be used to sensitize people to their own need for a personal relationship with Jesus Christ. Home study groups will find videotapes ideal. Women in a neighborhood would gravitate to the home of someone who would provide a comfortable setting, show the film, and then be open to sharing what had been learned through that session. Pastors often counsel young couples in preparation for marriage who are not believers. Sometimes one of the couple is a Christian, the other is not. This kind of video is excellent for sharing key messages in a way that is attractive and appealing. At the same time it often opens the conversation so Christ can be presented.

There is no way that this book can even scratch the surface in the vast numbers of opportunities that are available. The market is flooded with new titles, new productions, new opportunities. Materials are being produced faster than any of us can assimilate them. The hope is that you will be stimulated and encouraged to investigate what is really available. Then let your own imagination and creativity take over. Look at your own community, your mission field. Visualize what God wants to do through media to win your segment of the world to Himself. Often our ministries are limited only by our lack of vision or our unwillingness to try something new. The opportunities are vast. The materials are available. Look for someone's felt need and take the person a tape.

Share a Tract

For years a very simple form of media has been popular with evangelistic Christians. Nearly thirty years ago I came into contact with the first person I had ever known who was really involved in a tract ministry. Everywhere he went he left a tract. When he ate in a restaurant, he always left a tract for the person who would clean off the table after dinner. At the barber shop he was prepared to share a tract with barbers and those waiting for haircuts. When he stopped at the cleaners or bought gas at the service station, you could guarantee that the person who waited on him would receive a brief message about Jesus Christ in the form of a tract.

By today's standards the tracts of yesterday may seem colorless and relatively ineffective in communicating the message. Still God has used them in powerful ways through the years. Today there are beautiful tracts on almost every subject—salvation, Christian life, doctrine, ministry, Christian citizenship, science, drugs, family, holidays, grief, handicaps, depression, alcohol, power for living . . . and they are available to be used by individuals and churches alike. Many churches have tract racks near the media library where members are encouraged to come and find an ideal tract for sharing with a friend or neighbor. Southern Baptists have designed a whole series of tracts called *Choice Creations.* The intent is these beautiful, full-color tracts can help churches share God's message of salvation, love, encouragement, and hope. They are available through the Material Services Department of the Sunday School Board, 127 Ninth Avenue, North, Nashville, Tennessee 37234.

Oldies But Goodies

There is certainly nothing new about the things discussed in this chapter. With the exception of videotapes, all of these media forms have been used effectively through the years. Unfortunately, they have been used by too few people. Media library workers have known the value of books, tapes, and tracts for years. Pastors have handed out books to counselees when the occasion arose and often been pleased with the results. Church members who wanted to share their faith have used tracts at various times and in various ways through the years. But far too often our understanding of media as one of the most effective tools God has provided his people for evangelism has been limited.

For the most part we have not taught our people to use

these tools. Many pastors do not look upon their media library and the people who staff it as a resource for church evangelism. The average church member would have little concept of the ideas expressed here, never realizing the value of sharing a tape of the pastor's message with a next-door neighbor or passing a tape on marriage and the family to that friend who needs real help in that area. Every reader has a friend or friends who are walking through times of grief and hurt, but it has never dawned on many of us that we have resources available to us that would be tremendous helps. In the process a seed, a word, a hope could be sown that would ultimately open a life for Jesus Christ.

Our intent here is to stretch your thinking, enlarge your vision, encourage your dreaming new dreams. With the media available to you today, how could you use it to share Jesus Christ?

Notes

1. Dick Innes, *I Hate Witnessing* (Ventura, California: Regal Books, 1985), p. 124.

2. Ibid., p. 125.

3. Ibid., p. 148.

4. Robert Evans Ornstein, *Multimind* (Boston: Houghton, Mifflin Company, 1986), pp. 26-27.

9
Can You Imagine?

Dan Griffin is my kind of pastor! The pastor of the Cliff Temple Baptist Church in Dallas, Texas writes a weekly pastor's column in their church newsletter, *Kaleidoscope*. He calls his column "Graffiti." In the November 7, 1986 issue Dr. Griffin wrote:

"The reason I was able to give you Dr. G. Henton Davies' voice Sunday was because our audiotape library has virtually every worship service and revival service we've had in the last thirty years.

"Perhaps you'd like to request a taped message from the past. Just call 942-8601, and for $2.25 it's yours. We also have a good many videotapes of our television ministry.

"Sunday night I mentioned that any good Bible student is going, eventually, to want to invest in a good set of Bible commentaries. But you don't have to do that if money is a problem. We have an excellent selection of commentaries in our library. You may go there any time during library hours and browse.

"That's what I did at the seminary when I didn't own a set of commentaries. I did my studying in the seminary library.

"I want to encourage and facilitate your becoming an excellent student of the Bible.

"The only thing that will make a lasting change for good in your life is daily, growing contact with Jesus. If you don't know what he said and did, who are you trying to fool by calling yourself a Christian?

"Do not confuse having your name on the church roll with following Jesus as a daily disciple . . . or with actually being a CHRISTIAN. Big, BIG difference."

He's got it! I think he's got it!! This fine pastor obviously has seen the vision, has the message, knows the score, and is capitalizing on one of the church's primary resources . . . the media library. Right there in one spot are so many things that will help us do our jobs much better.

Can you imagine how much more effective the entire church family would be if they could share that pastor's understanding of the use of media in the context of sharing and growing our faith? That is the thesis of this entire book. God has given us tools, methods, and means to communicate His marvelous story, and it is our responsibility to use them all.

Certain media instruments are more obvious than others. In the previous chapter we discussed the "oldies but goodies"—the instruments that have been used effectively for a number of years. Now we want to look at some less obvious media that can be used with equal effectiveness. Remember! Media is any instrument, any method that can be used to communicate that message. Remember too that all of us are involved. Media isn't designated to one group of people in the church. You don't have to join the media library's staff to use media to share Christ. That's our old game that we often play. "Oh, media? I'm not interested! I'm the pastor and I don't have time to fool with that. We have a media library staff who deals with that!" How sad. The brother is confused. If he communicates at all, he does it through media.

The other side of that coin is the people who work with books and tapes in the church and act as if their job is to get in their little compartment and control their turf. Sometimes the impression is left that if it doesn't involve the Dewey Decimal system or cataloging, it isn't media. Wrong! Media is all the tools we use constantly to communicate. Our task is to use media effectively and to use it often to accomplish our mission.

A New Look

The technology of our day has given media a new look. So many more opportunities are available to ordinary people today than just a few years ago. A good example of that is the use of various kinds of instruments which once were limited to professional operators. Now anyone can use them. Let me share some prime examples.

Christian Movies

Just a few years ago Christian movies were limited both in numbers and in use. Those being produced were primarily low-budget films designed for youth camps and training opportunities. As recently as the sixties and seventies, this was the only kind of movie really available.

In the last several years, however, a whole new medium has begun to impact the Christian community. James Dobson, the highly popular Christian psychiatrist, was a pioneer in the use of Christian films as an instrument that transcends the former stereotype. Dobson's films have been shown across the country in almost every kind of setting. At first they were shown only in special settings primarily at church. But as his message of hope for marriages and families began to catch on, the variety of his audience and the location of the showing of the films greatly changed. Dobson's films have been shown everywhere—coliseums, civic centers, neighborhood clubhouses, fellowship halls, private homes.

And the make-up of the audiences has been widely varied. Non-Christians have been interested in Dobson's films. As previously noted, people tend to listen to that person who is scratching where they itch. Since Dobson

deals as a trained professional with key interests of this
era, his message is one unbelievers are willing to hear. In
the process Dobson clearly gives a witness to the necessity
of Jesus Christ's being Savior and Lord if a home is to be
what it should be. It may be years before the full impact
of this kind of sharing can be adequately measured.

With the advent of Dobson's films, the accessibility the
public had to those films, and something as simple as more
availability to projectors and more people able to run
them, the film revolution is in full swing. Film series by
such popular speakers as Chuck Swindoll, Tony Campolo,
Josh McDowell, Dawson McAllister, Tim Timmons, and
Kevin Lehman are now readily available. They range in
topic from marriage and family to vocation and commitment, aging, priorities, leisure, attitudes, the uniqueness
of the Bible, the reliability of Scripture and Messianic
prophecy.

The use for these excellent films is almost as broad as
your imagination. Last spring I was in a revival in a church
in North Carolina. The pastor took me by the Family Life
Center around 4:00 PM to speak to a group of children.
I spoke briefly and then joined them for a while as they
watched the children's film "The Lion, the Witch, and the
Wardrobe," based on C. S. Lewis's *Chronicles of Narnia.*
As we prepared to go to another meeting, I asked the
pastor about the children. "How many of these kids come
from Christian homes, Jim? How many of them have no
church background?" His answer could have well been
typical for many children today.

"This is a latch-key club, Don. These children come to
us straight out of school. Their parents both work and
need someplace for them to stay. I would say 90-95 percent of these children have no relationship with the
church whatsoever except the time they spend with us!"

Wow! What a tremendous opportunity! Young, recep-
tive minds being exposed to the gospel in an attractive,

creative way. The setting is totally nonthreatening and, without a doubt, the Father will use that to do a work of grace in some of those children's lives. Some of them will be the starting place God uses to reach entire families.

For a number of years churches have realized the importance of speaking to special groups in the life of the community. One church near a Baptist university recognizes each year certain groups: teams, student leadership, clubs. These groups are honored in church services and recognized for the importance of their contribution in the life of the college and the community. Other churches have done that type of thing with high school groups. I served in a church once where the church honored the athletic teams with a special banquet in their honor. At that time the team members were made to feel welcomed, appreciated, needed in the life of the church. Often a Christian athlete invited teammates to worship with him in the church that had hosted them. It was an important and effective ministry.

For many churches, especially those in large, urban communities, that kind of event is largely a thing of the past. For one thing, there are too many schools involved. In most urban and suburban churches six or seven different high schools are represented in the membership. The same is true with junior highs and colleges. Because the schools no longer have deep ties to communities as they did when the community was smaller and everyone came from that particular setting, there is no real desire on the part of school leadership to see their students feted in this manner.

Our church has discovered that there are ministries available, however, that have the same kind of impact. Little League teams thrive in both urban and rural communities. Often these teams are composed of children from every aspect of the community . . . rich and poor, churched and unchurched. And their parents are eager for them to have a positive experience. When the season is concluded, there is a need for some sort of get-together or celebration, but there is often real difficulty in finding an appropriate place for that to happen.

That's where the church comes in. Fellowship halls are ideal for that kind of meeting. We invite the league that plays nearest our facilities, offer to provide children and parents with a hot-dog meal and a movie that features the exciting plays and Christian testimony of some of America's most famous athletes. There are a number of movies available that fit this bill. Once again the possibilities are unlimited. We have discovered that people who would never attend church for any reason and who are closed to the sharing of the gospel come with much anticipation and excitement to that kind of meeting.

This kind of approach can be used with multiple groups. Thousands of churches have basketball and softball teams. Most of those teams have some sort of recognition banquet at the end of the season. Often these teams are composed of a composite of people . . . faithful church members who are dedicated Christians, peripheral members whose relationship to Christ is a bit shaky, and lost people who are associated with the team only because it gives them a chance to continue their athletic interest as adults. In other words, thousands of churches have a built-in evangelistic opportunity playing ball for them twice a week during the season. Certainly the church should explore every possibility to reach those who are at their doorstep, or perhaps we should say in their dug-out. So why not seize on an opportunity such as a sports banquet to share Christ through media?

Films such as *Champions,* featuring athletes Walter Payton, Madeline Mims, Roger Staubach, Alberto Salazar, Jeff Kemp, Betsy King, and many more are excellent for this kind of occasion. *A Man and His Men* (Word), the story of Tom Landry and the Dallas Cowboys, still impacts athletes mightily as the coach shares what Christ means in his life and ultimately in the lives of the men he influences. *Superstars on Location* (Word) is a film that takes a look at some of America's greatest professional sports heroes. These athletes share in an intimate fashion what brought them to Christ and how they are dealing with living and growing in the Christian life. The message of a film could well be the tool that many Christian leaders are looking for to reach that person who seems indifferent to other forms of media.

Sports is not the only subject in which people are interested. How about sex? The secular movie industry will testify to the fact that people by the millions will pay whatever to see movies on sex. Why not capitalize on that interest and introduce those needy people to Jesus?

Many churches have get-togethers of some kind for their young people after a Friday night football game. They also have summer lock-ins. There is no better time to invite lost teenagers to church than on one of these occasions. Often a Christian young person will lament, however, that there just isn't any interest on the part of their peers in coming to an event at the church. That changes quickly when their friends learn that a movie dealing with one of their favorite subjects is being shown. Maybe it would be good to start with Josh McDowell's *The Sexual Puzzle.* From there his series *Live Laugh Love* is a natural. That covers the whole spectrum of love, dating, and sex.

In his own humorous style McDowell, who has spoken to more college campuses than any speaker in history, deals with the "old" and "new" values of our culture. Sex without love and marriage without commitment are often the "new" norms of our fragile culture. McDowell contrasts those values with the concepts taught in God's Word and the values of our Judeo-Christian heritage. It's all done in a way that relates to where young people are these days. It just could be that a Christian film is the best evangelistic tool available for touching the lives of many young people.

It is impossible to list all the resources or all the possibilities available. That's your job! God's Spirit enlightens our minds and inspires us to recognize the particular need and the unique tool that is available in our own situation. The desire here is to "get the juices flowing." Think! Think of all the ways that the medium of Christian films could be used to reach your mission field. Think! Pray! Then get on it! People need Christ, and God has given you marvelous tools to reach them.

Turn the Radio On

Recently I was driving to a meeting at the church. The radio in my car was tuned to a local sports show. The program was one of those call-in shows where people telephone the host and give their opinions about the topic being discussed. I was engrossed in what was being said since the topic of the evening was how the various teams would fare in the upcoming Atlantic Coast Conference basketball season. People are wild about basketball in the Carolinas. They were calling from everywhere.

As could be expected, the talk show was interrupted occasionally by advertisements and on the hour by the national news. Each time a break came, however, the talk show host would instruct, "Now stay tuned. We'll be right back to hear what Dean Smith or Jim Valvano thinks about this issue." The response after each break made it obvious that people were staying tuned.

One break caught me completely off guard. A pleasant voice began to talk about lives that are filled with stress. The speaker illustrated with a humorous illustration or two and made the point that all of us were pushing too hard and running too fast. I thought to myself, *He's been reading my mail!* Then he went on to say that life becomes unbearable without the peace, purpose, and strength that is provided only by Jesus Christ. You could have knocked me over with a feather! This had not sounded like a religious message. He had hooked me with an appeal to common needs, made me laugh at myself, and then "wham!" He said what our world needs to hear . . . powerfully, poignantly, persuasively, and pointedly. His last words were, "This is Joe McKeever, pastor of the First Baptist Church of Charlotte."

I wonder how many people heard. They were still calling in when the break was over. How many? Five thousand? Ten? How many people were listening to that same sports show and heard the message of Christ and were "hooked" before they knew it just like I was? How would God use that message in the lives of those who heard? Would He plant in that moment a seed that would be watered by friends, and sometime down the way reaped to the glory of God? I've got to believe that's exactly what will happen.

Radio is a powerful instrument. It's with us everywhere we go. Driving, jogging, cleaning house, in the shower . . . we listen to radio. Advertisers tell us that no medium is so widely used. People of every walk of life listen regularly to radio. What a perfect instrument to creatively, effectively use to share our Lord's good news.

This is being done in hundreds of ways. Christian radio is increasingly popular. One only needs to look at the overwhelming success of Chuck Swindoll's "Insight for Living," John McArthur's "Grace to You," and James Dobson's "Focus on the Family" to realize that. Interestingly, these programs are heard and taken seriously by thousands of unbelievers. You see, they deal often with topics of interest that everybody wants to hear. There is no way to know how many people who did not know Jesus Christ have been led to a relationship with the Savior because a Christian friend shared with a neighbor how much a Christian radio program was blessing his or her life. In turn, that neighbor began to listen and the rest is history.

There should be a pointed effort in every one of our churches to use radio as one of the mediums that we employ to get out the message. Maybe it is as simple as providing through our media libraries the time schedules of well-known programs with a word of encouragement to our members to alert their non-Christian friends to the value of listening to these powerful speakers. Take one step forward and publish brochures with those time schedules. Sometimes the programs themselves will send all the brochures you want. Distribute those to church members with the challenge of "getting the word out."

Some churches will want to do more. Hundreds of our fellowships have radio broadcasts weekly. Some are broadcasts of our morning services. Others are devotionals by the pastor early in the morning or late in the evening. These are good instruments. Unfortunately they become too often simply routine, geared primarily to people who are already Christians, lacking in creativity and newness. If a church has this form of media already in place, maybe it would do well to form a media committee who could feed in fresh ideas, stimulate, encourage, and explore, so that new ways of reaching your community could be found. Then certainly there are those churches who have the resources to do something positive in the area of advertising, spot announcements, and devotionals that are geared to that unenlisted, unconverted listener. When this kind of radio is done well, nothing is more effective.

Paper Advertisements

Do you ever read the Saturday morning church page? You know, that's the segment of Saturday's paper where all the churches advertise what's taking place at the church the next day. There is a picture of the pastor, some wording such as "The Difference Is Worth the Distance" that serves as the church slogan, and the hours that the services will be held. Sometimes the pastor includes his sermon titles.

In many papers that ad costs substantial dollars. I often wonder who reads it. I mean, besides the people who go to church every Sunday and just want to see what their ad looks like.

There are at least three kinds of church growth. There is *biological growth*—the children who are being born into your church. We experience *transfer growth*—the people who move and transfer their church memberships from one church to another. And we have *new growth*, or *conversion growth.* This refers to the people who come to know Christ and then become part of the church family. It is that middle group that gets most of our attention.

In our services we hand out visitors' cards that have several responses on them concerning how the visitor arrived at our church. Did a friend bring them? Did they come because the church was recommended to them? Included in that list is "paper advertising" and "yellow pages." An interesting discovery has been that a fair amount of visitors come to our services because they read an ad on the "church page" (we have a very small one there weekly) and because they had seen our ad in the yellow pages of the phone book. I was particularly interested in the category of people who found us because of these ads. Where do you suppose they would fit in the categories of growth? To the person they would be classified as transfer growth. Church people who are looking for a new church home often go to those places for information. Great! That validates the use of church pages and yellow pages.

What about the unchurched? What about the lost person? What does he look for? When he reads the paper, what does he read? He reads the sports page. Maybe the movie ads, the TV listings. Women may read Erma Bombeck and Ann Landers. But they probably do not read the "church page."

Newspaper advertisements are highly effective when they are done correctly. The primary question that needs to be asked before they are used is, "Who are we attempting to reach with this message?" Like every other medium, the best use demands clear identification of the target group.

Some time ago our church decided to make a serious attempt to reach the lost and unchurched in Charlotte through the medium of the paper. To do that we identified the people we were attempting to reach. They were the people who make up the southeast quadrant of our city. A study was made of their characteristics. This group could be categorized as affluent, upper middle class, professional people. They are young. Many would be classified as "Yuppies." The people of this area are transient, rootless, lonely. While they value the family unit very highly, many of their homes are coming apart at the seams. Over 50 percent of Southeast Charlotte is single. Over 50 percent go to no one's church.

With that kind of profile, what message do we send? Traditional, "churchy" messages with stained-glass language and pious platitudes simply would not cut it with this group. So our leadership got their heads together. We got the help of a sharp public relations group who were very astute in putting images and messages together. We identified some graphic needs . . . the toll of climbing the ladder of success, crumbling marriages, rearing children in a day of declining morals, alcohol and drugs, workaholism and neglect of family, and loneliness. Once that was completed we began to design the message we wanted our community to hear from our church.

We were concerned that the lost person hear a message

of love, concern, caring. The attempt was made to call attention to an alternate life-style without moralizing or putting down. Our intent was to let the reader know that we knew the problems that beset his life, that we identified with his plight. But we knew answers that he must have to be a complete person.

The ads were placed in the least obvious place in the most widely distributed paper. The favorite haunts of the lost person's reading habits were invaded. The places that were normally "off-limits" to the church and a Christian witness were the very places we chose. Sports, entertainment, society—all those places where that person who is empty gravitates to in order to try and fill up that void— were the locations of our ads.

The success of the initial advertising campaign has been phenomenal. We ran six ads successively. Every two weeks there was a new advertisement appealing to a new segment of the unchurched population. To say that it raised our community's consciousness level of our church and its ministry would be a vast understatement. People came from everywhere. Following every advertisement calls came from people wanting to know about our ministries to divorcees, singles, youth, and preschool. I received a letter one day from a lady who lived nearly two hundred miles away. She said, "I am walking through a divorce. It is the most painful thing I've ever experienced. I cannot do it without someone who cares. When I read your ad in the *Observer,* I knew that I had to come to your church. Soon I will be moving to Charlotte and I'm coming to Carmel."

Newspaper advertising is a medium that needs to be investigated by the church. As always, we need to use those things at our disposal that are going to speak to our generation. Since that original campaign our church has continued with this attempt to speak to our community. It is still working with much effectiveness.

LIFE DOESN'T HAVE TO BE EMPTY.

Sometimes people face special stresses. As when their children first go out on their own. We try to help those under any special stress. And encourage them to rediscover the fullness of life. Join us Sunday. At a church that believes in a full life for everyone.

CARMEL BAPTIST CHURCH

2101 Carmel Road • Charlotte, N.C. 28226 • Phone (704) 366-9100
Sunday Services at 9:30 and 11 a.m. and 6 p.m.

THE FALLACY OF THE FRIENDLY DIVORCE.

Nobody wins when a marriage ends. If you know too well the pains of separation or loss, a new support group is waiting inside our doors.

CARMEL BAPTIST CHURCH
2101 Carmel Road • Charlotte, North Carolina 28226 • Telephone (704) 366-9100
Sunday Services at 9:30, 11:00 and 6:00.

Maximize Mail-Outs

For many years churches have been mailing materials in an attempt to communicate a message. Do you realize that all the mail that goes out from your church is just media being used to convey a message? Our problem often comes at the point of "doing more and more for less and less." One lady said to me, "Our church sends out so much 'stuff' that when I see it's from the church I throw it in the trash." That church just struck out!

Mail costs too much to waste our efforts. At the same time, few instruments have more potential for good than the medium of mail. Several years ago a friend mentioned to me that their church was using direct mail as an evangelistic tool. We discussed what they were doing. They had planned a series of meetings dealing with the home and family and had sent invitations to a large group of people who lived in the area surrounding their church. I was quite interested and later inquired about the project. It had gone extremely well. There had been many visitors, a number of additions to the church.

At that time we gave direct mailing some real consideration. But our budget was limited and we felt unable to pursue it at that time. Some time elapsed before we were trying to figure out how we could invite a large segment of our community to join with us for our Christmas cantata. That holiday season we had decided to use music as a medium for reaching people. Instead of something warm and beautiful, geared entirely for our own people, we had made a commitment to music designed to convey the Christmas story in an evangelistic way so the person without Christ might come to know Him through that concert. But there was one catch. We must figure out a way to get the lost person there.

Direct mail was the answer. Our people decided that we would invite everyone in a four-mile radius of the church. We drew up the invitation, had it printed, went tʊ a direct mail company, and started the ball rolling. Included in the invitation were instructions to call and reserve a seat for the performance. Who would have guessed the response?

Our phone began to ring. The calls were almost over-whelming to our secretarial help. We added additional volunteers to help us in that area. Quickly that perfor-mance filled up with people who had never even been on the grounds of Carmel Baptist Church.

That was the beginning. Since that time our perfor-mances have grown to three at Christmas and Easter. An orchestra has been added. But the message is still the same. Christ Jesus came that sinful, alienated humans might have a personal relationship with God. Christ died for our sins and rose that we might have life, eternal and abundant. The media is still the same too. We continue to use direct mail to bring in the folks who will be blessed through the medium of music. We always have overflow-ing crowds.

A new medium has been added this year to the whole process. For some time we have given the concertgoers an opportunity to buy an audiotape of the performance. Yearly we have sold large numbers. But this year we will *give* everyone a tape. Since we have always registered our guests, obtaining their names, addresses, and phone num-bers, it is easy to add a new ministry. This year we will take a copy of the beautiful gospel message that they have just heard into their homes. It will be a reminder of a meaningful evening that they enjoyed. Also, it will give us a chance to get into that home and, hopefully, tell them of that Christ our choir sang about. There would be no comparable way we could go into many of these homes as a welcomed guest who is providing them with a wanted gift. Obviously the key to all we do is media . . . music, tapes, and direct mail.

Mail can be used many other ways evangelistically. Our

church visits newcomers. A list giving us addresses and names is secured. We send a warm letter of welcome with a notice that someone from our church will soon be by to welcome them personally and to give them a gift. Then follow-up teams go with packets that include community telephone numbers, a map of the area, and other items of interest including a gift from our church such as a pot holder with the logo of the church or a cookbook created by our members. We are received with surprising warmth and appreciation. Often this contact through mail leads to a permanent relationship both with the church and her Lord.

New mothers love this attention! We use mail to contact the ladies who have just given birth to a new baby. We send them a note of congratulations with a promise to visit soon and give their new babies a gift. Once again a follow-up team goes to that home with a cute bib for the baby, a book for the mother, and an invitation to come to Carmel Baptist Church. Quite often that new mother is open and waiting for someone who will tell her about the love of God in Jesus Christ. Numbers of new mothers have been won through this technique.

Now let's take a look in the next chapter at the best medium that God has ever provided to assure us of His message of love.

There have been a large number of churches who have written asking about using the ideas for newspaper ads that we have produced. The production of these advertisements was costly. We continue to produce new ads. In an attempt to recoup some of the expenses and provide excellent material for sister churches, we are offering two sets of seven ads each at $500 per set. To get your set write: Dr. Robert Reccord, 2101 Carmel Road, Charlotte, North Carolina 28226.

10

God in My Skin

A number of years ago Bill Turner, now pastor of the South Main Baptist Church in Houston, Texas, told a story that has never left me. In one of the worship services at a recreation conference at Ridgecrest, Turner told of a little black boy who was growing up in the Watts section of Los Angeles. It was in the sixties when all across America angry riots were taking place. Watts had been hard hit. As the mother prepared to put her son to bed, she said his prayers with him, pulled up the covers, kissed him good night, turned off the light, and started to leave the room. Suddenly he said, "Mom! Mom! Don't leave me here. I'm afraid!"

She smiled and reasoned, "Honey, you don't have to be afraid. There's no reason at all to be scared. Don't you know that God is right here with you?"

The little boy puckered up to cry and then said, "Mom, I know God is here. But I need someone with skin on!"

We all do. We need someone with skin on to help us over the hurdles of life. If we know Jesus, we know that He is right here. But we still need someone with skin on to model for us what His love is all about. What about those who don't know Him? How do they come to know Him? Someone with skin on touches their lives, loves them, walks with them, tells the good news of Christ in their times of sharing. Inevitably it is that person with skin

124

on who becomes God's best medium to bring hope into the life of that separated one.

The medium is the message! How true. Can you think back with me to the people who have touched your life? People who have made all the difference? Once Jesus was walking through a crowd of people and a very needy woman reached out to touch the hem of His garment in hopes that just touching Him would somehow cure her ailments. Jesus stopped, turned around, and asked, "Who touched me?" That's a key question. All of us should check that out periodically. Who has significantly impacted our lives? Equally important is the question, Why?

When I review my own pilgrimage, some people "jump out" in my memory as the media God used for me. Let me share my impressions of a few of them.

Brother Howell. I grew up in the First Methodist Church of Waco, Texas. My mother was a committed Christian who loved her church and was actively involved in it. My dad was a nominal church member who rarely attended but insisted that the family be in church on Sunday morning while he got some things done at home. I suppose that my ten-year-old mind was stimulated by the large, balding, bespectacled man who was my pastor because I had never been conscious of a male figure who was really committed to Jesus Christ. It was so evident to me that he was a "real guy." He loved sports, had an undying commitment to his SMU Mustangs, was an outdoorsman, and still loved Jesus supremely. His life was an instrument. Through it came the message that one can be a real man, a strong man, and God's man . . . all at the same time.

Mr. X. Would you believe that someone could deeply touch your life for Jesus Christ and you would not even know his name? It can happen! Take my word for it. In my teenage years I went to my parents with a desire to leave the old downtown church where I had grown up to join a suburban church where all my friends attended. I wanted to play basketball with my buddies on their excellent church team. My parents had some reticence, but I suppose they feared a drifting away from the church on my part. So reluctantly they let me go.

Our Sunday School teacher that eighth-grade year left a deep impression on my life. Though I cannot remember his name, I remember him. The way he related to a group of rowdy, rude, indifferent, lost boys was something I couldn't understand then. In retrospect I just remember with amazement that He loved us! In spite of the way we acted, he loved us. Week after week he loved us. That message sunk deep into my subconsciousness. Though I was many years from the level of understanding that would let me identify the dynamic that took place there, somehow I recognized that here was a man willing to put up with all the "guff" that age group can hand out simply because Jesus Christ was real in his life. He, too, was a vehicle, a conduit through which the love of God flowed to my parched life. He was a medium used to broadcast God's love for teenage boys.

Mr. H., Senior High Choir. What a place for a witness. Who would have guessed that a slight, artistic, kind chorus teacher would have had a primary influence on a guy whose only apparent interests in life were football and girls? Mr. H. was there in those key moments when God was ready to do his work of grace. I came to know Jesus Christ personally as a senior in high school. While the particular moment when I opened up my life and asked Jesus to enter was completely away from the place where I met Mr. H. daily, I strongly suspect that he had watered the seeds sufficiently for the event to become a reality. I had heard about Jesus. In his life I saw Him.

Brother Jim. One of our common mistaken ideas is that we are reborn full grown much like Diana out of the head of Zeus. We see that acted out constantly in the context of the church. Let a guy get saved, get baptized, be in the church a month, and we give him a job leading RAs. If he sticks around for a year, is active on Sunday and Wednesday night, and survives the RAs, we make him a deacon. Our idea seems to be that we get saved and quickly thereafter are full grown. Not so! Growth is a lifelong proposition. Some of my most significant years of growth followed high school, college, seminary, pastoring, serving as a chaplain in the army. God allowed me as a thirty-year-old to walk daily with a man who was my peer chronologically but who became my father in the ministry.

If someone asked me what was so important about our common walk, I would have to say that in his life I saw the glory of God. We are often invoked in Scripture to "give God the glory." I doubt that most of us know what that really means. When I give God the glory, I structure my life so that it becomes a channel. Through it God can reveal to others who he really is. Brother Jim was willing to be that medium. As I watched him deal with people who were tough to love, on his knees in the quietness of his study, in homes where he told so winsomely the message of Jesus to those who were alienated from the Father, leading his staff with firmness and love, I saw the Father. He gave God the glory.

I hope you have been thinking as you read. This is my story. What's yours? What persons did God choose to be the media, those key persons "with skin on" who would touch you? Surely there were those people. Somehow there always are those people whom God uses just for our lives. I thank God for them.

You're Next

That's important for you to know. Equally important is the awareness that God wants to use you now. You're next. He has used others to impact your life, and now there is someone waiting for you to be the instrument, the medium, the person who "gives God the glory."

When Jesus walked the sandy shores of the Sea of Galilee He undoubtedly knew that His ministry would soon come to an end. He couldn't continue to preach His radical message of love and live a long, happy life. Death was inevitable, so He drew around Him a select group out of the multitude that had been following Him and took them up on the mountainside to serve as "spiritual bodyguards" while He went deeper into the hills to pray.

Mark 3:13 draws the picture for us: "He went up on the mountain, and called to him those whom he desired, and they came to him" (RSV). Out of the larger group He called twelve men. These men were to be His apostles. Later these same men would be called disciples. Jesus had His message and His method. Through these disciples He would take the Roman world and shake it until its "teeth rattled."

It was through His disciples, His students, the learners of His way that a world lost and searching for an unknown God would know of the Father's love for them. Jesus had chosen His disciples and they would teach others, disciple others. The faith of the Carpenter would spread. Lives would be changed. Old things would become new. A God who had been before only an abstract entity, a sort of oblong blur, now would be alive and vibrant.

The disciples Jesus chose were to be students. They would sit at the feet of the Master and learn His ways. But, more important, they would know Him. They would mimic the characteristics, assume the values, act out the life-style of the One who taught them about life.

Strange, isn't it, how things change. It all started with only twelve disciples and now across the world there are millions claiming to be disciples of the Fisherman. But somehow things have changed. Words have taken on new meanings, new concepts have arisen, and millions of His followers today don't understand what it means to be a disciple. Many of us who are called to be His disciples are fuzzy and unclear about what discipleship means.

Our situations can be like an experience that Norman Vincent Peale once had. It seems that Dr. Peale's custom whenever he went into a new community to speak was to buy a local newspaper, read it, become familiar with some local news, and, if possible, use that for illustrations in his sermon. One summer he was asked to come to Bloomington, Illinois. It so happens that Bloomington has two small communities nearby named Normal and Oblong. Dr. Peale picked up a Bloomington paper and read, "Normal Boy Marries Oblong Girl." He could hardly wait to use the caption in his sermon. He sprung it on his congregation and there was absolutely no response. They were too used to the names "Normal" and "Oblong." They were overly familiar with those towns, and the illustration had no impact at all.

Many of us who are His followers today are like that. We want to be His disciples. But we don't really know what that means. We have never seriously examined the lives of those first disciples to determine the qualities which set them apart. Nor have we investigated the biblical requirements for discipleship and the implication of those standards in our own lives.

God Calls Us

Jesus calls us to be His disciples. Jesus originally chose twelve men to form that band of believers. But through the pages of history his call has been to all people. That's interesting! The Son of God needed a method that would allow His message to continue. He knew that His preaching had been effective, but he also knew that He would soon be gone. He had to find a way of making His message permanent. So He chose people. They would be His channel of communication.

That may not sound unusual. We are familiar with that idea. But be aware that there are those who think God preferred other ways. Islam teaches that God dropped the sacred book out of the sky. In it were the teachings of Allah. The Mormons are taught that Joseph Smith found golden tablets buried. The stress, of course, in both illustrations is something that occurred magically, mysteriously. The deity revealed Himself without involving people.

Not so with the God of the Bible. Yahweh used people. Jesus chose men. Most were plain, uneducated men. His choice was men with no theological training, no ecclesiastical or political importance. They were men of varying backgrounds, men of different understandings of life, different hopes and dreams. He chose men who only had one thing in common . . . they loved Him.

The Gospel of Mark gives two reasons for appointing the twelve.

(1) *They were to "be with him."* It's not too difficult to plan an ideal social order, a new way of life when it's only in your imagination. Plato created an ideal republic. Thomas Moore imagined a utopia. Bacon conjured up in his fertile mind a new Atlantis. But Jesus *established* the Kingdom of God with real people, real flesh and blood.

The disciples were "with him" and they were very human. They interrupted His prayers with their immaturity, delayed His plans with their personal ambition, disturbed His most important discourses with their bickering. But still they were Jesus' choice.

(2) *They were "sent forth."* These disciples, with all their humanness, were "sent forth" with the pivotal message of all human history. Jesus had written it on their hearts. They had been with Him and now they could tell a world begging for love that the God of all the ages loved them. They were sent to show the rejected, the lonely, the misfits, the mixed-up, the left-out that they were OK. God had created them, but in the process of life they found

themselves broken. Now the Creator had initiated a relationship that would provide a way for healing that brokenness. He had provided a way to be re-created. Jesus "sent forth" people that they might be "truth through personality." Humanity is the "stuff" which God chose to use as his primary media.

God Calls All Kinds of People

One of the fantastic things about Jesus is the wide spectrum from which His messengers were chosen. Remember who they were:

Simon the Zealot—The political radical. This man was a member of the political party of that day who considered themselves "the agents of God's wrath." (The radical 1960s produced the Black Panthers and the Weathermen. Today a similar group is the Lebanese Armed Revolution Faction.) Like these extremists, the zealots of Simon's persuasion felt they had been singled out for one purpose—the overthrow of the government. They hated anyone connected with the Roman government. There was a particular bitterness toward those Jews who had compromised their race by helping the Romans. Jesus called Simon.

Matthew the Tax Collector—The most hated of men. Matthew was the kind of man that Simon hated most. He was a Jew who had gone to the Roman government and asked for the privilege of taking taxes from his own people. (He had to pay Rome a certain amount, but since he could set the amount he charged the people, he would always set it high enough that he got more than his share.) He was a rich man, but no one was more despised by his peers.

Peter the Fisherman—Hardly in the social class of Matthew. Peter was a man with the charisma of a leader. Men gladly followed this big man. Successful in the fishing industry of his area, he laid it all down to follow the Galilean.

But that same impulsive nature that caused him to give it all up to follow Jesus would later motivate him to deny his Lord.

Judas the Fiscal Conservative—He was a man concerned with money. Judas was a man more concerned with the drachma and the way it was spent than he was the people who were blessed by its spending. He was a mystery man, alone, never really loved by the group. Judas was the man who never seemed to grasp those things that Jesus infused into the lives of those who walked with Him.

Strange bunch! What a mixture of people! Jesus loved them all. He called them to be His disciples. Do you see that Jesus called from every background, every walk of life? He called men with varying personalities, interests, understandings of life. That has never changed. The Lord still calls all sorts of people. Christianity is that strange mixture of people who have a unity in commitment but a vast diversity in the way that commitment is expressed.

There is a great need today for people . . . all kinds of people . . . who love Jesus and are willing to be his instruments to reach this complex world we live in. Jesus never forced people into some kind of quaint little mold. He encouraged the freedom to think different thoughts, to look at life from different vantage points, to express thoughts differently. Read Christian history and that becomes so evident. Think of the men and women from every culture, every ideological background, who were unified only in their love and commitment to Jesus Christ. Picture, would you, people like these:

William Booth—great founder of the Salvation Army who loved people who were down and out and knew their hope was Jesus Christ.

Billy Sunday—the professional baseball player turned evangelist who shared his love for Jesus Christ with fire and enthusiasm and called thousands of people to a relationship with his Savior.

Charles Colson—President Nixon's "hatchet man" who found Christ through crisis and gave his life to prison reform and ministry to the incarcerated.

Dietrich Bonhoeffer—the brilliant theologian who, like the apostle Paul, celebrated his relationship with Christ from a prison cell.

John Wesley—founder of the Methodist Church. He preached for sixty-four years. In 42,300 messages, an average of fifteen messages a week for fifty-four years, he proclaimed Christ. He traveled the equivalent of twenty times around the globe sharing the Good News, and he did it all on horseback or walking.

Billy Graham—the angular evangelist from North Carolina who has preached the simple gospel to more people than any man in history.

Albert Schweitzer—physician, master musician, theologian, philosopher, one of the intellectually elite of Europe, who gave his life to Christ in darkest Africa.

What an unusual mix of people. Like those first disciples, Christians through the ages have been vastly different, yet unbelievably alike. Our common ground is Jesus Christ. Our common task is the sharing of His message. God calls all kinds of people!

God Calls Us to Action

Love is something you are. But it is also something you do. Several years ago a survey was taken and the question was asked, "Who loved you when you were between the ages of seven and ten?" Once that was answered a second question followed, "How do you know they loved you?" The answers to the second question were all the same. Those being questioned answered, "I knew because that person did something!"

We know that people love us when their love motivates

them to action. Interestingly enough, their love in turn often motivates us to action. I love Gordon McDonald's book *Restoring Your Spiritual Passion* (Nelson, 1987), in which he talks about five kinds of people who help us keep the fires of our spiritual lives burning. The first group he identifies are the people he calls VRPs, very resourceful people. Everyone has known the kind of person McDonald is referring to. They are the mentors, the encouragers, those people in our lives who touch us on the deepest level of human relationships. They excite our spiritual passion. They motivate us to be more than we imagined we could be.

The kind of person I'm describing is often a parent, a grandparent, someone in the family who pours love our way from the earliest days of our life. Many times they are the coaches, the teachers, Sunday School leaders, the pastor . . . people who take time to get involved with us. Later our peers, our professors, our marriage partners become VRPs for us. But without exception the persons who impact our lives are people who do something. We see and we hear in their lives something of value, something that we want to be in our lives.

That's how God uses media! He speaks! He shows! The ideal medium that God continues to use can perform both of those methods. That medium is the finest instrument God has to appeal to the logical, analytical mind of the left-brain thinker. The same medium is God's premier tool for graphically portraying his message to the intuitive, the artistic, the picture-oriented right-brain thinker. The best medium God has is people . . . you and me.

Many people have heard that God loves them. Now they need to see it. They need to see God in our skin.

Mediagraphy

These titles have been selected by the author and personnel of the Church Media Library Department, Baptist Sunday School Board, to assist in witnessing.

Books for Witness Training

Bennett, Dave. *Keep Giving Away the Faith*. Nashville: Convention Press, 1980.

Chafin, Kenneth L. *The Reluctant Witness*. Nashville: Broadman Press, 1975.

Chamberlain, Eugene. *When Can a Child Believe?* Nashville: Broadman Press, 1973.

Crawford, Dan R. *EvangeLife: A Guide to Life-style Evangelism*. Nashville: Broadman Press, 1984.

Hogue, C. B. *Every Christian's Job*. Nashville: Convention Press, 1980.

Larson, Muriel. *Ways Women Can Witness*. Nashville: Broadman Press, 1984.

Miles, Delos. *Overcoming Barriers to Witnessing*. Nashville: Broadman Press, 1984.

Thompson, W. Oscar. *Concentric Circles of Concern*. Nashville: Broadman Press, 1981.

Turner, Chip. *The Church Video Answerbook*. Nashville: Broadman Press, 1986.

Books to Use in Witnessing Situations

Blackburn, Bill. *Understanding Your Feelings*. Nashville: Broadman Press, 1983.

Blair, Joe. *When Bad Things Happen, God Still Loves*. Nashville: Broadman Press, 1986.

Carter, James E. *Facing the Final Foe*. Nashville: Broadman Press, 1986.

Claypool, John. *Stages: The Art of Living the Expected*. Waco: Word Books, 1977.

Cole, Douglas. *When Families Hurt*. Nashville: Broadman Press, 1979.

Dobson, James. *Dr. Dobson Answers Your Questions*. Wheaton: Tyndale House, 1982.

Geddes, Jim. *The Bright Side of Depression.* Nashville: Broadman Press, 1985.

George, Denise. *Dear Unborn Child.* Nashville: Broadman Press, 1984.

Grange, Robert. *Origins and Destiny: A Scientist Examines God's Handiwork.* Waco: Word Books, 1986.

Hauk, Gary H. *Building Bonds Between Adults and Their Aging Parents.* Nashville: Convention Press, 1987.

Herring, Reuben. *Becoming Friends with Your Children.* Nashville: Broadman Press, 1984.

Knorr, Dandi Daley. *When the Answer Is No.* Nashville: Broadman Press, 1985.

Richards, Robert Eugene. *Heart of a Champion.* Old Tappan: Fleming H. Revell, 1959.

Audiocassettes

Duvall, Evelyn. *Coping with Kids.* Nashville: Broadman Press, 1975.

Dye, Harold. *Aging Is Better than You Think.* Nashville: Broadman Press, 1982.

Martin, Francis A. *Facing Grief and Death.* Nashville: Broadman Press, 1981.

Suggestions for the Class Leader

Preface

Use a slide-tape presentation which illustrates a busy pastor—demonstrates an active library that supports the pastor in the tasks shown and concludes with a segment based on Matthew 9:36-38 (NIV) demonstrating how the library staff and media can help in evangelism.

Make a brief statement (based on slide-tape presentation) as to why this book was written.

Introduction

Use a poster to list examples of God using media.

Definition of media at bottom of above list—covered with a strip—revealed and discussed after discussion of God's use of media.

Share an actual (personal if possible) experience of someone "reached" with media. Emphasize the *importance* of a verbal witness and explain how media can support and supplement that verbal effort.

Poster Idea:

God Used Media

1. Burning bush
2. Writing on Belshazzar's wall
3. Tablets of stone
4. Prophets who acted out His message

5. Songs sung by the singer, David
6. Message wrapped in human flesh

Media
"Any means, agency, or instrumentality; specifically, a means of communication that reaches the general public . . ."

or, for our purposes:

"Media is any way, any instrument, any vehicle that one employs in the sharing of the gospel with the general public (lost world)."

Chapter 1, Sharing the Message

Use an overhead cel showing outline of chapter.

After revealing all of the outline, cover all but one heading discussing each and revealing each, one at a time.

Repeat the definition of media.

The "What" of Media
Use handout, "The Media Tree" (see page 147).

Share verbally several types of media and briefly discuss how each of these can be used in communication.

The "Why" of Media
List on the chalkboard some advantages of using media in evangelism as suggested by conferees.

Use overhead cels to reveal the list of advantages of using media. Use strips to reveal these advantages one at a time to compare with the list on the chalkboard.

Overhead cel idea:
Chapter 1, Sharing the Message
The "What" of Media
The "Why" of Media
The "Where" of Media
The "Who" of Media

Overhead cel idea:

Advantages of Using Media

1. Enables more people to witness
2. Influences more readily than the word of a stranger
3. Demonstrates a genuine interest in persons
4. Gives a reason for a return visit
5. Provides topics for conversation
6. Reminds a person of the church's interest in him
7. Expands the capability of the visitor
8. Suits the convenience of the prospect
9. Provides a way to relate to the entire family
10. Overcomes a lack of religious background

The "Where" of Media

Lecture using personal experiences (if possible) of the Holy Spirit's leadership in selection of person to be visited and in selection and use of particular media.

The "Who" of Media

Enlist persons before the conference to read the following passages of Scripture and lead conferees in discussion:

Genesis 3:14-15

Isaiah 9:6-7

Isaiah 53:2-6

Use overhead cel of quote of John Stott (discuss).

Lecture on "Jesus" is the "Who."

Overhead cel idea:

First, He sent His Son. Then He sent His Spirit. Now He sends His church, that is, us. He sends us out by His Spirit into this world to announce His Son's salvation—He worked through His Son to achieve it; He works through us to make it known.

—John Stott

Chapter 2, Tell It Often, Tell It Well

Use overhead cel showing outline of chapter. Reveal each heading one at a time.

Enlist a conferee before the conference to share the author's proposal experience, emphasizing: What if no one was there?

What if no one cared?

What if no one could understand?

Enlist another conferee to relate the experience of the 18-year-old boy in revival, emphasizing:

His girlfriend doesn't understand;

The boys on the next day don't really hear.

Teacher gives a verbal summary of above. Use arrow to point to each of these as discussed.

Speak so all may hear

Emphasize "all"—underline on cel during conference

Relate personal experiences of witnessing to "all" types.

Poster of 1 Corinthians 9:22 (The Living Bible)

Ask for personal interpretations of this Scripture by a few conferees.

Speak so all may hear . . . and listen

Verbally relate the author's story about the missionary and the bum.

Return to overhead cel listing advantages of using media. Emphasize #3, #7, #10.

Reemphasize 1 Corinthians 9:22.

Speak so all may hear . . . and understand

Overhead cel of brain.

Share briefly the author's information about the brain and different personalities.

Share examples (personal if possible) of witnessing with media to: (List on chalkboard)

Accountant and Artist
Mechanic and Sculptor
Carpenter and Designer

Overhead Cel Idea:
Chapter 2, Tell It Often, Tell It Well
Speak so all may hear
Speak so all may hear . . . and listen
Speak so all may hear . . . and understand

Poster Idea:
1 Corinthians 9:22
(Letter the Scripture text here.)

Chapter 3, Old Testament Models

Discuss "Show and Tell" and how it relates to use of media in evangelism.

Conference leader reads and explains Scripture passages.

Use overhead cel with outline of chapter—Lecture.

Overhead cel idea:
Situational Messages
Prophetic Messages

Chapter 4, God's Best Message

Use lecture method.

Discuss verbal and visual methods used.

Jesus:
   Visual: Mustard seed, lilies of the field, farmer sowing seed
   Audio: Speaking from boat, Storyteller

Discuss how messages should be designed to appeal to both left-brain persons and right-brain persons.

Use overhead cel to illustrate "Kerusso."

Discuss the importance of using every means possible to communicate the gospel.

Overhead cel idea:

Kerusso

or

Communicate

Communicate the Gospel

Chapter 5, Jesus, the Master Communicator

Relate story of "The Complacent Sower."
List on chalkboard:
Jesus' Methods of Communicating
1. Used contemporary methods
   a. Storytelling
   b. Parables
   c. Healing
2. Used language of the people
3. Developed new methods
   a. Writing in sand
   b. Raising the dead
Discuss Triple Brain
1. R-complex
2. Limbic system
3. Cerebrum - left and right
Conclusion: We should mimic the Greatest Communicator.

Chapter 6, Communication Is The Name of the Game

Give a verbal summary of introduction to the chapter:
1. Pastor and "Jesus music"
2. Poor results today in evangelism
3. Much of the problem is in poor communication
Use overhead cel—Communication by Jesus and Disciples
1. They understood their audience
2. They adapted to their audience
Use overhead cel and briefly discuss:
   Who's got the key

Give me another handle
Using overhead cel, explain "Selection Categories."
Group Sharing of experiences (personal if possible) in using media in relating to "deep needs."

Opening that Lock
Close chapter with emphasis on the power of the Holy Spirit to "break through" the filtering process.

Overhead cel idea:
Chapter 6
Communication Is the Name of the Game

How and Why People Hear Messages
1.   Selective Exposure
2.   Selective Attention
3.   Selective Comprehension
4.   Selective Distortion
5.   Selective Retention

Chapter 7, A Cure for Stopped-Up Ears

Use overhead cel showing outline of chapter.
Cover all of cel except chapter number and title.
Share author's introduction concerning ear plugs.
Ask conferees to suggest some "Plugs" of today that hinder persons from hearing the gospel. List these on the chalkboard.
Reveal chapter outline (through "Busy Routines") and group the "Plugs" suggested by conferees according to chapter outline:
Secularism
Mastery and Self-Sufficiency
Amusement and Diversion
Busy Routines
Reveal on overhead cel "Pulling the Plugs." Give spe-

cific examples (personal if possible) of "Pulling Plugs" with media.

Overhead cel idea:

Chapter 7

A Cure for Stopped-Up Ears

Secularism
Mastery and Self-Sufficiency
Amusement and Diversion
Busy Routines
Pulling the Plugs

Chapter 8, Keeping On Keeping On

Use overhead cel showing outline of chapter. Cover all of cel except chapter number and title. Share introduction of chapter in teacher's own words with illustrations. Reveal headings of outline one at a time.

Give Them a Book

Review for the conferees (with as much detail as needed) the author's examples for each circumstance.

Divide conferees in twos. Let them decide how they individually will use this approach at home with specific persons and circumstances in mind. Hear reports from as many of these as time will allow. Encourage discussion of new circumstances.

Take Them a Tape

Briefly lecture on author's material.

View a portion or all of the videotape, "Before You Say 'I Do . . .' "

Discuss the possible uses of this tape. Demonstrate this on a small portable VCR-TV unit that could be used in door-to-door evangelism.

Share a Tract
Distribute Tract TripPaks with sample *Choice Creations* tracts and order form.

Ask conferees for suggestions as to the use of these tracts.

Discuss how the media library can get involved in this ministry.

Oldies But Goodies
Verbally "sum up" the chapter.
Overhead cel idea:
       Chapter 8, Keeping On Keeping On
Give Them a Book
Take Them a Tape
Share a Tract
Oldies But Goodies
Overhead cel idea:
       Chapter 8, Keeping On Keeping On

Give Them a Book
1. Where there is a death or dying—give a book.
2. Where there is separation or divorce—give a book.
3. Where there are personal needs—give a book.
4. When a personal interest is discovered—give a book.
5. Where there are children—give a book.

Chapter 9, Can You Imagine?

Use overhead cel showing outline of chapter.

A verbal summary of the author's introduction with special emphasis on Dr. Davies' material if any of the conferees are pastors or other church staff members.

A New Look
Summary statement.

Christian Movies
Lead conferees in a discussion of the use of motion pictures in evangelism.

Review the material on pages 49 and 50 of *Media on the Move: Reaching Out with Resources* concerning the use of motion pictures with the bus ministry and mediamobiles.

Show a portion of "The Sexual Puzzle" and lead a discussion as to how it could be used in witnessing.

Turn the Radio On

Paper Advertisements

Maximize Mail-Outs
Briefly summarize the author's message in these last three areas.
Overhead cel idea:
                    Chapter 9, Can You Imagine?
A New Look
Christian Movies
Turn the Radio On
Paper Advertisements
Maximize Mail-Outs

Chapter 10, God in My Skin

Use overhead cel with following outline:
Persons Who Have Influenced My Life
You're Next
God Calls Men
God Calls All Kinds of Men
God Calls Us to Action
Reveal this outline all at one time. Use an arrow to walk through outline.

Teacher gives testimony of persons who have influenced his or her life.

Ask for testimonies from conferees.

Move arrow to "You're Next." Have a conferee prepare before this session to read Mark 3:13.

Verbally describe how God used ordinary persons.

Move arrow to "God Calls Men." Share with conferees how this differs from "Islam" and "Mormonism."

Share with conferees the author's two reasons why Jesus appointed the twelve.

Move arrow to "God Calls All Kinds of Men."

Have four conferees prepared to share concerning: Simon the Zealot, Matthew the Tax Collector, Peter the Fisherman, and Judas the Fiscal Conservative.

Share verbally concerning: William Booth, Billy Sunday, Charles Colson, Dietrich Bonhoeffer, John Wesley, Billy Graham, and Albert Schweitzer.

Move arrow to "God Calls Us to Action."

Close conference by sharing the need for *all types* of persons using *all kinds* of methods (emphasing the use of media) to win *all types* of persons to Jesus.

"The Media Tree," referred to on page 138, is available on request from Church Media Library Department, Baptist Sunday School Board, 127 Ninth Avenue North, Nashville, Tennessee 37234.

The Church Study Course

The Church Study Course is a Southern Baptist education system consisting of short courses for adults and youth combined with a credit and recognition system. Also available in the system are noncredit short courses (called foundational units) for children and preschoolers. The courses in the Church Study Course are for use in addition to the ongoing study and training curricula made available to churches by the denomination.

More than 500 courses are available in 23 subject areas. Courses are flexible enough to offer credit for either individual or group study. Credit is awarded for each course completed. These credits may be applied to one or more of the 100 plus diploma plans in the system. Diplomas are available for most leadership positions as well as general diplomas for all Christians. These diplomas are the certification that a person has completed from five to eight prescribed courses. Diploma requirements are given in the catalogs.

"Enrollment" in a diploma plan is made by completing Form 725 "Church Study Course Enrollment/Credit Request" and sending it to the Awards Office at the Sunday School Board. Course credit may also be requested on this form. A permanent record of courses and diplomas will be maintained by the Awards Office. Twice each year up-to-date reports called "transcripts" will be sent to churches to distribute to members participating in the Church

148

Study Course. Each transcript will list courses and diplomas completed and will show progress toward diplomas currently being sought. The transcript will show which courses are needed to complete diploma requirements. A diploma will be issued automatically when the final requirement is met.

Complete details about the Church Study Course system, courses available, and diplomas offered may be found in a current copy of the *Church Study Course Catalog* and in the study course section of the *Church Materials Catalog*. Study course materials are available from Baptist Book Stores.

The Church Study Course system is simple enough to be administered by volunteer workers with limited time. The system is universal so that credit earned in one church is recognized in all other Southern Baptist churches. Approximately 600,000 awards are earned by adults and youth each year.

The Church Study Course is promoted by the Sunday School Board, 127 Ninth Avenue, North, Nashville, Tennessee 37234; by Woman's Missionary Union, P.O. Box C-10, Birmingham, Alabama 35283-0010; by the Brotherhood Commission, 1548 Poplar Avenue, Memphis, Tennessee 38104; and by the respective departments of the state conventions affiliated with the Southern Baptist Convention.

How to Request Credit for this Course

This book is the text for course number 21026 in subject area: "Church Media Library Leadership." This course is designed for five hours of group study.

Credit for this course may be obtained in two ways:
   1. Read the book and attend class sessions. (If you are

absent from one or more sessions, complete the "Personal Learning Activities" for the material missed.)

2. Read the book and complete the "Personal Learning Activities." (Written work should be submitted to an appropriate church leader.)

A request for credit may be made on Form 725 "Church Study Course Enrollment/Credit Request" and sent to the Awards Office, Sunday School Board, 127 Ninth Avenue, North, Nashville, Tennessee 37234. The form on the following page may be used to request credit.

A record of your awards will be maintained by the Awards Office. Twice each year copies will be sent to churches for distribution to members.

CHURCH STUDY COURSE
ENROLLMENT/CREDIT REQUEST (FORM-725)

INSTRUCTIONS

1. Please PRINT or TYPE
2. COURSE CREDIT REQUEST — Requirements must be met. Use exact title
3. ENROLLMENT IN DIPLOMA PLANS — Enter selected diploma title to enroll
4. For additional information see the Church Study Course Catalog
5. Duplicate additional forms as needed. Free forms are available from the Awards Office and State Conventions

PERSONAL CSC NUMBER (If Known)

TYPE OF REQUEST (Check all that apply)

- Course Credit
- Enrollment in Diploma Plan

- Address Change
- Name Change
- Church Change

REQUEST FOR

- Mr.
- Mrs.
- Miss

Name (First, MI, Last)

Street, Route, or P O Box

City, State, Zip Code

DATE OF BIRTH

Month	Day	Year

CHURCH

Church Name

Mailing Address

City, State, Zip Code

COURSE CREDIT REQUEST

Course No	Use exact title
21026	1 *Ears to Hear, Eyes to See*
	Use exact title 2
	Use exact title 3
	Use exact title 4
	Use exact title 5

ENROLLMENT IN DIPLOMA PLANS

If you have not previously indicated a diploma(s) you wish to earn, or you are beginning work on a new one(s), select and enter the diploma title from the current Church Study Course Catalog. Select one that relates to your leadership responsibility or interest. When all requirements have been met, the diploma will be automatically mailed to your church. No charge will be made for enrollment or diplomas.

Title of diploma	Age group or area
1.	

Title of diploma	Age group or area
2.	

Signature of Pastor, Teacher, or Study Leader	Date

MAIL THIS REQUEST TO

CHURCH STUDY COURSE AWARDS OFFICE
RESEARCH SERVICES DEPARTMENT
127 NINTH AVENUE, NORTH
NASHVILLE, TENNESSEE 37234

FORM-725 (Rev 7-83)

Personal Learning Activities

Chapter 1

1. Develop your own definition of "media," relating the concept to *communication* and *evangelism*. Write your definition on the lines below.

   _____
   _____
   _____
   _____
   _____

2. Why is it important to emphasize the use of media in evangelism?

   _____
   _____
   _____

3. Explain why a consideration of how God communicates with His people is basic to the study of media in evangelism.

   _____
   _____

4. Cite evidence from both Old and New Testaments that Jesus is God's instrument of redemption and should be the focus of our message.

Old Testament	New Testament
(1) _____	(1) _____
(2) _____	(2) _____

Chapter 2

1. What is the key to telling well the story of Jesus?

   _____

   _____

   _____

2. In what ways other than geographically may the "all" in the Great Commission be applied to our outreach with the gospel message?

   (1) _____

   (2) _____

3. Identify two ways churches may show sensitivity in sharing the message.

   (1) _____

   (2) _____

4. Recall what you have read about the two-brain theory. Contrast the abilities usually found in the right-brain thinker to those of the left-brain thinker.

   Right-brain thinking   **Left-brain thinking**

   _____   _____

   _____   _____

   _____   _____

   Name two kinds of media which would appeal to the right-brain thinker.

   _____

   _____

   Which forms of media would be more appealing to the left-brain thinker?

   _____

   _____

5. How does an understanding of the two-brain theory become important in choosing media to convey messages?

   _____

   _____

   _____

Chapter 3

1. God's use of verbal and visual communication to relay messages to His people in Hebrew history may be called a "situational" model. Give three examples of situational messages in the Old Testament.

   (1) _____

   (2) _____

   (3) _____

(2) God's use of *persons* to relay a message to His people may be called a "prophetic" model. What are two examples of prophetic models from the Old Testament?

   (1) _____

   (2) _____

Chapter 4

1. Jesus used a variety of methods in communicating with people. List three examples of these.

   (1) _____

   (2) _____

   (3) _____

2. Compare the Greek words *kerusso* and *martureo* in relation to proclaiming the gospel.

   Kerusso means _____

   Martureo means _____

   The lost man must both _____

   and _____ in our lives the message of salvation.

3. How is modern technology important to contemporary proclaiming of God's Word?

   _____

   _____

   _____

Chapter 5

1. Consider your position as minister, teacher, leader, or media library staff person. Relate the parable, "The Complacent Sower," to your efforts in effectively communicating with media the gospel message. State a specific action you could take to increase your effectiveness.

   _____

   _____

2. Identify four situations in which people heard Jesus' message because He communicated with their *needs*.

   (1) _____
   (2) _____
   (3) _____
   (4) _____

3. According to the triple-brain theory, which kind of response is produced by each segment of the human brain? Match the type of response with the appropriate brain segment.

   Brain segment   **Response type**
   ____R-complex   1. Intellectual
   ____Limbic   2. Instinctual
   ____Cerebrum   3. Emotional

4. Give an example of how Jesus considered each area of response in reaching people.

   Area of response   **People Jesus reached**
   personal comfort: _____
   feelings: _____
   thinking: _____

5. In what way did Jesus' conversation with the woman at the well sustain her attention without alienating her from His message?

   _____

   _____

   _____

6. How did Jesus appeal to the feelings level of His hearers in the Sermon on the Mount?

_____
_____
_____

Chapter 6

1. Jesus and His disciples provide ideal models for contemporary communication in that they _____ their audience and _____ to that audience.
2. Match the way our minds can filter out information heard to the response in our reception.
    Filter System
    ____Selective exposure
    ____Selective attention
    ____Selective comprehension
    ____Selective distortion
    ____Selective retention
    Response
    a. We remember what we want to remember.
    b. We listen to what we want to hear.
    c. We may, in hearing, change the message to what we want it to say.
    d. We understand, of what is heard, what our biases allow us to hear.
    e. We respond to what we want to hear.
3. The key to successfully sharing an idea is to
    _____ _____ _____ _____ of the hearer.
4. What is meant by "felt needs"?

    _____
    _____

    What are two kinds of felt needs?
    (1) _____
    (2) _____

Identify some felt needs among the people you encounter in your area of church service.

_____

_____

_____

5. In *Communication Theory for Christian Witness,*
   Charles H. Kraft lists factors usually involved in an
   adequate communication of the gospel message. Iden-
   tify with a check mark (√) those factors below.
   _____ Identification of felt needs
   _____ Dealing with felt needs
   _____ Sharing of news about persons' needs
   _____ Adopting a formal plan for communicating with
   persons in need
   _____ Discovering deeper needs
   _____ Dealing with deeper needs
   _____ Discovering and dealing with still more needs
6. What is the value of the mental filter system?

_____

In light of this value, how can closed minds be
opened?

_____

_____

Chapter 7

1. List four twentieth-century trends which often hinder
   the lost from hearing our message.
   (1) _____
   (2) _____
   (3) _____
   (4) _____
   Think about services in your media library. Are there
   specific actions which could be taken to minimize the
   effects of these trends on the lives of media library
   users? Note two or three of these actions below.

_____

2. The author states, "The same medicine doesn't work on all people." Note several ways in which people differ and therefore need a variety of programming.

3. How can the rise of large "super churches" be compared to the growth of the supermarket?

    What do these growth patterns show about diversity and reaching people?

Chapter 8

1. In times of personal crisis a book with a message of _____ can often open the heart and mind of that person who is experiencing trouble.

2. Below are felt needs relating to death and dying and suffering. Beside each stated need write the letter of one or more titles which could be used to reach a person facing that type of crisis.

    Crises

    ____(1) A parent has lost a child.

    ____(2) A grown child has lost a parent.

    ____(3) A person is experiencing a series of loss crises among family and friends.

    ____(4) A grieving person is confused over what he is feeling after a loss.

    Titles

    a. Ron Lee Davis, *Gold in the Making*

b. Granger Westberg, *Good Grief*
c. Joseph Bayly, *A View from the Hearse*
d. Warren Wiersbe, *Why Us?*
e. Joyce Landorf, *Mourning Song*
f. Martin Marty, *A Cry of Absence*

List other titles on suffering and death which you may have used in similar situations.

_____   _____
_____   _____
_____   _____

3. Several books which could offer encouragement or direction in dealing with marriage problems were mentioned in this chapter. From these titles or from titles in your media library, choose a source appropriate for each of the following situations. Write the chosen title below each stated situation:

(1) A young couple ask, "How can we make our marriage better?"

_____

(2) A wife complains, "He just won't talk to me."

_____

(3) A forty-two-year-old husband is troubled with feelings that his life is empty, and he wants to get away from it all and *live*.

_____

(4) A husband and wife express feelings of growing apart in their marriage.

_____

(5) A wife is confused and hurt by her middle-aged husband's change of personality.

_____

4. Browse your church media library or the shelves of your local Christian book store to find books concerning separation, divorce, or remarriage. From these titles or from those listed in this chapter, choose and

list three which could be helpful to a person going
through one or more of these situations.

(1) _____
(2) _____
(3) _____

5. Again, discover what is available in your church media
library and indicate one title which could be a resource in dealing with each problem.
(1) Job loss _____
(2) Choice of vocation _____
(3) Child discipline _____
(4) Adolescent rebellion _____

6. Before recommending a book or author, it is important to

_____
_____

7. Focus on a neighbor or co-worker or friend with
whom you want to share the gospel message. Think
about what is of great personal interest to that person.
   From your church media library, from personal
reading, or from the author's suggestions, choose one
or two titles which you feel you could use with that
person to open ears. Write the title(s) on the lines
below and indicate where you will secure the source.

_____
_____
_____

8. Concentrate on the children with whom your church
has contact. Think of a specific way which is not now
being used in your church to provide for the needs of
these persons. List below book titles or programs
which would be possibilities for witnessing.

_____
_____
_____
_____

9. After reviewing the suggestions in the section on audiocassettes, list three ways they can be used to minister to personal needs.

    (1) _____
    (2) _____
    (3) _____

10. Identify three ways videotapes may be used to sensitize people to their own need for a personal relationship with Jesus.

    (1) _____
    (2) _____
    (3) _____

11. Describe how the *Choice Creations* series differs from earlier tracts.

    _____
    _____

    Point out four ways these tracts may be used in witnessing.

    (1) _____
    (2) _____
    (3) _____
    (4) _____

    Where may these tracts be obtained?

    _____
    _____

Chapter 9

1. What reasons can you give for the popularity of the James Dobson films?

    _____
    _____

    Consider how your church might use such motion pictures in ministering to felt needs. Identify one target group which your church could try to reach with such films as these.

Write down a specific way your church could use motion pictures to reach this group.

_____

_____

2. Why is radio an effective instrument for sharing the gospel?

_____

_____

3. From your own listening experience or from this chapter, recall and write below two series from Christian radio.

(1) _____

(2) _____

How may a church media library promote the use of this tool?

_____

_____

_____

4. State the function of a mass media committee in the local church.

_____

_____

_____

5. Name three categories of church growth and explain what is meant by each.

(1) _____ _____

_____

(2) _____ _____

_____

(3) _____ _____

_____

Which of these categories is most likely to be reached by the usual church listing in a newspaper or yellow pages?

_____

6. Explain how the identification of a target group should affect the nature of the message chosen for an advertisement. To illustrate, use the author's example or one from your own concern for a particular group.

_____
_____
_____
_____
_____

7. Three methods of reaching people by direct mailing are
   (1) _____
   _____
   (2) _____
   _____
   and
   (3) _____
   _____

8. In planning for a newspaper message, four considerations to effect an on-target message are
   (1) _____
   (2) _____
   (3) _____
   (4) _____

Chapter 10

1. After reading the author's stories of people who touched his life, focus on a person or persons whom God used to influence your life. Write the name(s) below.

_____
_____

What lesson did you learn from this influence?

_____
_____

2. Give several characteristics of the twelve men Jesus chose to bear His message.

_____   _____
_____   _____
_____   _____

What two reasons does the Gospel of Mark give for Jesus' appointing these men?

(1) _____

(2) _____

3. Below are listed several other messengers Jesus chose. Find the characteristic which most nearly describes each and write its letter in the space beside the name.

_____ Matthew the Tax-collector

_____ Judas the Fiscal Conservative

_____ Simon the Zealot

_____ Peter the Fisherman

a. political radical

b. loner

c. despised rich

d. impulsive leader

What does this list say about the nature of the people Jesus calls to serve Him?

_____
_____

4. From modern Christian history name the men who served/serve in the following ways:

Service	Man
imprisoned theologian	_____
ball player turned evangelist	_____
founder of Methodist church	_____
multi-gifted person dedicated to service in Africa	_____
world-wide evangelist to the masses	_____
founder of the Salvation Army	_____
convicted politician turned prison reformer/minister	_____

5. We know that people love us when _____
    _____

6. Summarize in one sentence the value of God's best
    medicine—people—in communicating His message.
    _____
    _____
    _____

Appendix

The Advantages of Witnessing Through Media

Churches have in their media libraries many kinds of resources. These resources include books, recordings, periodicals, filmstrips, audiocassettes, and videocassettes that can be used in communicating the story of Jesus. There are many advantages to using a variety of media in witnessing to the lost and ministering to people.

1. *Enables more people to witness.* Anyone can share a book or a recording. After giving the title to a neighbor or friend, the visitor can say, "When you've finished it, I'll take it back to the church library." Following this plan might be the first step toward becoming a bolder witness.

2. *Influences more readily than the word of a stranger.* People are inclined to believe what they read. If they listen to an audiocassette or read a book by an expert, they are more likely to accept his statement than that of the visitor who may be a stranger.

3. *Demonstrates a genuine interest in persons.* The visitor will find himself thinking about people in a new way as he tries to discover a point of contact. Then when he returns several times, bringing media which relates to the interests and concerns of the person, the person will sense the sincere interest of "this Christian" in him.

4. *Gives a reason for a return visit.* The visitor will want to pick up the material to return it to the media library.

EARS TO HEAR, EYES TO SEE

Ideally, he will take another item of material with him to leave on this visit.

5. *Provides topics for conversation.* The use of media can give the visitor interesting topics for discussion in his continued contacts with the person rather than repeating comments such as, "We're sorry you didn't come to church last Sunday. I wish you could have come."

6. *Reminds a person of the church's interest in him.* A book has on the title page and the book pocket the name and address of the church library. While it remains on the coffee table, each time the person sees it he will be reminded that a member of the church came to visit him.

7. *Expands the capability of the visitor.* The visitor will not always have the knowledge or background to talk about every interest or problem that could arise. It is usually possible to find something printed or recorded that provides information that the visitor can use both in becoming familiar with the subject and in sharing information with the person.

8. *Suits the convenience of the prospect.* Sometime, after a visitor has been in a home for a short while, his "welcome" begins to "run out." His "timing" may be bad, especially if he came in the middle of a person's favorite program. When the person gets restless, it is time for the visitor to leave. A book or recording can stay and witness after the visitor has gone.

9. *Provides a way to relate to the entire family.* By bringing a book or a recording for the small child in the family, the visitor shows an interest in the child although the initial concern was for the parent. Through a variety of media, a visitor can have a meaningful ministry with an entire family.

10. *Overcomes a lack of religious background.* Many people have never been in Sunday School or church. They do not read their Bibles. Studying media in the home provides an understanding this person may need before

he is ready to talk about spiritual things and certainly
before he is ready to attend church. The visitor may serve
as a tutor using a variety of media as "customized" cur-
riculum materials.

The Visitor's Preparation

How does a visitor prepare for a forthcoming visit?
What aids will he use in helping him to record his visits?
What should he remember as he knocks on the door?

1. *Planning ahead.* The visitor who witnesses through
media must plan ahead. At church on Sunday or Wednesday he will need to go to the church library to find material that will relate to the prospect's felt needs. For
visitation to be effective, the visitor must think ahead
about those he will visit and secure the appropriate material. Library staff members who participate in this approach to witnessing can help visitors find appropriate
media.

2. *Keeping records.* The visitor should keep a record of
each person he has visited, the date of the visit, and the
title of the book, tape, recording, or other item of media
left with the person. (In this section is a suggested form.)
The form has a place to record the hobbies, other interests, and number of visits that have been made. Under
"Remarks," the material shared should be listed. Some of
the lines on the form can be used to describe the visit.
Other visits can be recorded on the remainder of the
lines.

This form provides a convenient way to keep a record
of the visits made, materials left, and responses obtained.
In addition, it provides an excellent way to evaluate
progress.

3. *Depending upon God.* After the materials are left
and the responses made have been reviewed, then de-
pendence must be made on the Holy Spirit to determine

VISITOR'S RECORD FORM

DATE	

NAME	BIRTHDATE

STREET ADDRESS	HOME PHONE

CITY	ZIP CODE

CHRISTIAN?   ☐ YES   ☐ NO   CHURCH MEMBERSHIP

OCCUPATION	BUSINESS PHONE

HOBBIES AND INTERESTS

PROBLEMS

FAMILY MEMBERS	AGE	CHRISTIAN YES	CHRISTIAN NO	CHURCH MEMBERSHIP	RELATIONSHIP

CONTACTS

DATE	REMARKS (MATERIALS USED RESPONSE ETC.)

CONTINUE ON BACK

if there has been too much or too little contact. Is it time to take something else? What other material or contact would be useful in continuing the approach?

The visitor who is witnessing for Christ needs to have a moment-by-moment relationship with Him. This kind of relationship puts meaning into all efforts to witness. By depending on the leadership of the Holy Spirit, a visitor leaves the results in God's hands.

A Plan to Promote Witnessing Through Media

Goals and actions should be determined. Basically, the needs are: (1) training of persons who are interested, and (2) providing media library support.

The goal for this program and possible actions could read:

Goal: To enlist and train _____ people to use media in witnessing.   (number)

  A. *Contact leaders for names of people who may be interested.* Presentations can be made in meetings with deacons, church council members, and officers and teachers.
  B. *Select initial participants.* After prayerful consideration, the initial prospective trainees should be selected. These people should be contacted personally and the plan explained to them.
  C. *Provide training.* Training opportunities should be provided for interested people to study this book. It should be continued for at least thirteen weeks or one quarter to give sufficient time to try the ideas and share experiences. Part of the training experience would include reviewing a variety of media and explaining the different circumstances where titles could be used tactfully and sensitively.

How to Develop a Media Education Program will be especially helpful in setting up and conducting the training. This booklet (available from the Materials Services Department of The Sunday School Board, 127 Ninth Ave. N., Nashville, TN 37234) gives step-by-step procedures for planning and conducting workshops to train persons in the use of media. At least two copies will be needed for each work group, one for the sponsoring group and one for the leader.

The Media Library Supporting the Plan

The visitor needs all the help he can get. How can the media library help him?

1. *Select new media for the basic collection.* Selecting materials which have the potential for use in witnessing is an important library function.

Materials should be placed in the library to relate to specific interests. The mediagraphy in this book lists examples of the type of materials that are usable. Care must be taken to ensure purposeful selection.

2. *Select media from the collection.* The library staff can assist the visitor in selecting material. The visitor will not be as familiar with the library's collection as the library workers. Therefore, when visitors come to the library and describe a particular situation for which they need appropriate media, it is helpful when a library staff member says, "How about this title?" This attitude on the part of the library staff saves time for the visitor and shows that the staff member is interested in helping in the media approach to witnessing. The staff member should try to avoid having to say, "No, we don't have it." If there is time and money, the library should offer to purchase requested items which are not in the collection.

Some of the best help in selecting media from the church media library for visitation can be given by the personal testimonies of library users. If some people have been helped through using media, many others probably will benefit from the same materials.

3. *Promote the use of media in visitation.* The church media library can use various ways to promote the use of library media in visitation. In any promotional effort, the target group is of prime importance. For example, displays and demonstrations can be prepared and used appropriately for such groups as deacons and officers and teachers.

The following suggestions may be used to promote related titles and new media additions in the library:

a. *Display media.* The media library should periodically set up displays including materials that are useful in witnessing.

b. *Use posters.* Posters are good to use in promotional efforts. Posters plant seeds as they serve to remind people of ideas which have been shared in other ways. A poster should be simple so that a person can get the message at a glance.

Place the posters in places where deacons, church staff members, and Sunday School workers will see them. Use general themes on the posters such as "share your library's media with others."

c. *Demonstrate ways to use media.* A demonstration is one of the finest ways to publicize the use of materials. For example: (The scene begins with a knock on the door. A man comes to the door.)

VISITOR: Hello, Mr. Jones. Remember me? I'm John Harvey. I was here to see you the other day and I've had you on my mind. While I was here, you shared a problem you were facing and I've been praying for you. Also, I went by our church library to see if I could find something that might interest you. I found this book and brought it along. I think you might enjoy reading it. I'll leave it with you and come back later to pick it up. Before I come back, I'll look around in the library again to see if I can find something else you might like.

d. *Prepare mediagraphies.* A mediagraphy is a list of books and audiovisuals related to a particular subject. These mediagraphies can be used to pinpoint media which the library has for use in visitation. Mediagraphies of materials including biography and fiction, and subject areas as the Bible and science, sports, hobbies, family life, Christian life, and doctrine would be especially helpful for visitors. These lists should indicate the age groups with which each different item could be used.

4. *Encourage use of paperbacks.* Paperbacks can be used to advantage in visitation. First, it is helpful to have multiple copies of some titles. Paperbacks are economical and enable the library to have several copies at minimum cost. There is very little work to processing extra copies since only one set of catalog cards is needed for all copies of a title.

Some people prefer to read a paperback rather than a hardback book. When properly reinforced with tape, paperbacks will last for many circulations.

5. *Offer a special circulation system.* The rules concerning the circulation of media used in visitation must take into consideration the special requirements of this program. Listed below are some exceptions to regular library rules which apply to media used in visitation:

a. *No fines.* No fines should be charged for overdue media checked out by a visitor for use in visitation. It would not be unusual for a month to pass between visits. Thus, to enforce a two-week loan period after which fines accumulated would seriously hamper the program. The worker on duty should select a date far enough in advance and write it on the date due slip and charging card. A potential difficulty is that, occasionally, a person to whom a visit has been made will return the item to the church media library. To avoid asking for an overdue fine, date the material in the usual way and then write the letters "nf" (no fine) by the date on the date due slip.

(2) *Special charging card for visitors.* It is recommended that a special card be prepared for the visitor to use to keep up with the media he is taking to people. The church can have cards printed for this purpose. (See sample card.)

The visitor then can keep these cards in his Bible or visitation notebook to remind him of when and where he has placed the material.

6. *Paying for lost material.* It is not always possible for the visitor to retrieve material that has been placed. The church, not the visitor, should pay for the loss. If possible, the material should be replaced by the library's purchase of a new copy.

7. *Alter media library hours to accommodate visitors.* Hours that the library is open may have to be altered to accommodate the needs of those who use media in visitation. If a church has a regular time for visitation, the library should be open at least thirty minutes before the set time to begin visiting. This schedule will give those who failed to plan ahead an opportunity to select media.

The greatest need is to involve people—interested people—in witnessing through media. The suggestions made in this appendix are only ideas to be used or adapted as needed. Leaders are encouraged to use their own creativity as they plan and implement this approach.

SUB-LENDER'S CHARGING CARD

NOTE: TO BE RETAINED BY SUB-LENDER.

Last Name of Author	Accession No.
Book Title	

LOAN DATE	NAME (Use extra line for address or phone as needed)